From Tsars to Commissars

The Story of the Russian Revolution

Russia's past was steeped in violence and intrigue. Under the reign of the early Tsars the barbaric practice of serfdom developed and her people were enslaved. When Karl Marx and Friedrich Engels offered a blueprint for action and an ideology in their Communist Manifesto the class struggle began. This story penetrates the century-long barrier of mystery and suspicion and reveals the cultural heritage, the dominant personalities, and the social and political upheavals that have made the Soviet Union one of the most powerful nations in the world today.

FROM TSARS TO COMMISSARS

The Story of the Russian Revolution

by Kaye Moulton Teall

Maps and Drawings by Barry Martin

JULIAN MESSNER • NEW YORK

Published by Julian Messner
Division of Pocket Books, Inc.
8 West 40 Street, New York 10018

Printed in the United States of America
Library of Congress Catalog Card No. 66-14000

To My Son

From Tsars to Commissars

The Story of the Russian Revolution

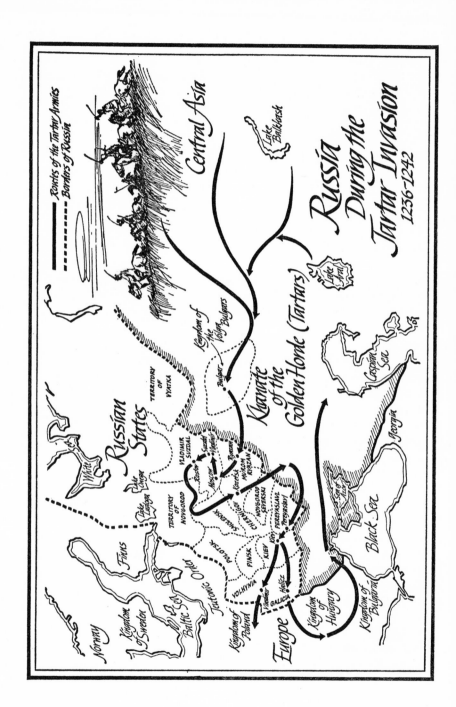

Russia
During the
Tartar Invasion
1256-1242

★ ONE

IN THE VILLAGE OF COYOACAN, A SUBURB OF MEXICO CITY, August 20, 1940, dawned bright and clear despite the fact that it was the middle of the rainy season. Leon Trotsky, Russian exile and arch-enemy of Joseph Stalin, arose promptly at seven and threw back the heavy steel shutters which barred the morning sunlight from his bedroom.

"Another lucky day," he said to his wife, Natalia, "we are still alive."

He had been saying it each morning since May 24, that horror-filled night scarcely two months before when the last attack on his life had been made. He had been awakened by blasts of machine-gun fire cutting through the bedroom in which he now slept. He and Natalia had saved themselves by simply rolling off the bed and partially under it, using it as a shield between them and the bullets.

With more than three hundred rounds of ammunition expended in little more than three minutes, it was a near miracle that he and Natalia had escaped. Seva, their ten-year-old grandson, sleeping in the next room, hadn't been quite as lucky. His big toe was grazed by a bullet which cut through the bed he had occupied only seconds before. Of the two incendiary bombs thrown into his room by the fleeing attackers, one had proved a dud and Natalia had been able to smother the other with a blanket.

The attackers, disguised as Mexican policemen, left as suddenly as they had appeared, taking with them the young American whose job it was to guard the Trotskys' bedroom door. The other guards, penned in the outside guardhouse

9

and menaced by machine guns, watched them all leave, noting that the American, Harte, seemed to go along without much resistance. Was he part of the mob, they wondered? Had he been bribed to let the attackers inside the house after they had overpowered the outside guards?

It was a question only Harte himself could have answered and he was to have no opportunity to explain his actions or to defend himself. Weeks later, the Mexican police, still painstakingly tracking down clues, found Harte's beaten and bullet-ridden body covered with a layer of quicklime, buried beneath the floor of an abandoned farmhouse.

Trotsky himself was not as interested in the killers as he was in the forces behind them. He had long ago learned the lesson that every hunted man must sooner or later face: there are always men whose twisted minds and trigger fingers may be bought or frightened into carrying out another's violent plans.

And that other, Trotsky was certain, the man who had masterminded the attack on him, was Joseph Stalin, the dictator of Communist Russia. He was equally certain that the failure of this attempt would not stop Stalin. He had a strange, unexplainable premonition about when the next attempt would come.

"He will try again," Trotsky predicted, "when Hitler's attacks center more attention on England."

Twelve weeks ago, the German blitzkrieg of Great Britain had been speculation only; now, on August 20, 1940, it was a reality. Hitler's bombers were pounding the dauntless British almost constantly.

But the sun was shining in Mexico, the air was sparkling clear. Trotsky turned from the window.

"You know," he told Natalia, "I feel well this morning, better than I have felt for a long time."

The only clouds were low on the horizon, dark, hovering close to the distant volcanoes, almost out of sight.

The day proceeded along the ruts of established routine. Trotsky fed his rabbits and chickens, petted the family dog, spent several hours at his desk, all within the high walls which surrounded the villa. The guards made their quiet rounds, one remaining always in each of the three towers from which the electronic gates to the inside were controlled, towers so tall that they overshadowed even the ancient trees shading the villa. Now and then the glint of the sun on the metal buttons of the uniformed guards or the gun emplacements along the twenty-foot-high wall gave a sinister note to the bright day, hinting, but only briefly, at the horror that was to come.

At five o'clock, Trotsky, Natalia, and several members of the staff, including Joseph Hansen, who served in the dual role of secretary and guard, gathered in the dining room for the customary tea. During the conversation, Hansen returned to a favorite scheme of his, that of searching visitors for weapons before allowing them inside the gates.

"No," Trotsky said once more. "Either we trust people and let them in without a search or we do not admit them at all."

The whole idea of living in a fortress was repugnant to him.

"It reminds me of the first prison I was in," he told Hansen. "The doors make the same sound when they shut. It is not a home; it's a medieval prison."

But to be suspicious of every friend who called, to make them submit to the indignity of a search for hidden weapons? —Trotsky shook his head. He could not bear the thought.

He finished his tea and went back to the garden. Joseph Hansen returned to the roof near the main guard tower to work on an addition he was making to the general alarm system.

It was about 5:20 when the guards were alerted by the arrival of a Buick sedan near the front gates. They looked it over, then relaxed. It was only Frank Jacson, a man they knew as the husband of the American girl, Sylvia Agelhoff, a devoted friend of Trotsky and the sister of his former secretary. Since his introduction to the Trotsky household a few weeks before, Jacson had become good friends with several of the guards, lending them his car and doing favors for them. Trotsky himself had not cared particularly for the man but he tolerated him for Sylvia's sake.

Jacson called up to the guards. "Has Sylvia arrived yet?"

"No," Hansen answered him. He had not known that Jacson and Sylvia were expected but it was not unusual for Trotsky to forget to tell him things like that. The massive steel gates swung open and Jacson stepped inside where he was met by Harold Robins, another guard. Robins escorted him to the rabbit hutch, where Trotsky was sorting out dry forage for his pets.

Jacson spoke first to Trotsky, then turned and raised his hat to Natalia, who stood on the balcony of the dining room. He walked toward her as they exchanged friendly greetings.

"I'm frightfully thirsty. May I have a glass of water?" he asked politely.

"Perhaps you would like a cup of tea?" she offered.

"No, no."

Natalia frowned as she noticed the raincoat draped over his arm. "Why are you wearing your hat and topcoat?" she asked. "It's so sunny today."

Jacson pressed the coat more tightly against his body. "Yes, but you know it won't last long. It might rain."

He seemed unusually nervous, she thought, as she got the water for him.

Trotsky noticed it, too, as Jacson fumbled among some papers he was carrying. "Your health is poor again. You look ill. That is not good," he told Jacson.

There was a pause while Jacson produced an article he was writing which Trotsky had promised to look over and check for statistics. Glancing at the sheaf of typewritten pages, Trotsky began slowly to remove his work gloves.

"Well, what do you say, shall we go over your article?" he asked. He brushed absently at his blue jacket and started toward the house. At the door of his study, he stopped and motioned his visitor through.

Trotsky rested his arms on the desk and, lowering his body into the chair, directed his attention to the manuscript in front of him. Placing his raincoat casually on the edge of the desk, Jacson moved to stand at Trotsky's left.

As Trotsky began to read, Jacson silently and carefully drew from the pocket of his raincoat an alpenstock, a short pickax of the type used by mountain climbers. Its handle had been cut down so that it was no longer than the seven-inch steel blade, which had a claw hammer on one end, a sharp point on the other. Moving with studied casualness behind Trotsky, the six-foot, sturdily built Jacson raised the weapon and brought it down with all his strength on the back of Trotsky's head.

Trotsky's animal cry of agony chilled the bone marrow of all those who heard it. Jacson, who had undoubtedly expected him to die instantly, was almost completely demoralized by its sound. As Trotsky rose from his chair like a gore-covered ghost, the back of his head completely crushed, his brain penetrated by the steel point, Jacson grabbed him. Trotsky bit his restraining hand with all the strength that was left in him, then fell, stumbled, and tried to rise. Half-crawling, half-running, he headed for the door, Jacson following, pulling at him, hysterically trying to deal the blow that would end the nightmare.

Shaken and terrified by the hideous scream, the guards on the wall could see through the window the figures of two men struggling and recognized Trotsky's blue work jacket. Inside the house, Natalia started blindly in the direction from which the cry had come. Joseph Hansen burst through the door of the dining room. Trotsky staggered out of his study, blood covering his face and soaking his shoulders.

"See what they have done to me!" he cried as Robins and Natalia burst through the north door. As Trotsky made his way to the balcony, Natalia threw her arms around him. "What happened, what happened?" she sobbed.

Trotsky's voice was calm, almost everyday. "Jacson," he said simply, then slumped and Natalia eased him to the floor.

The two guards sprang for Jacson, who stood just inside the study, dangling a pistol in his limp hand, gasping for breath. "You take care of him," Hansen told Robins. "I'll see what's happened to the Old Man."

Hansen hurried toward Trotsky and Natalia as Robins took the gun from Jacson and hit him over the head with it.

"What happened?" Hansen asked Trotsky.

"Jacson shot me . . . I am seriously wounded . . . I feel that this time it is the end," Trotsky answered laboriously.

"No," Hansen told him, "we didn't hear any shot. He struck you with something."

Trotsky pressed Hansen's hand in reply and spoke to Natalia in Russian. As she found a pillow and placed it under his battered head, he touched her hand to his lips. Later she found some ice and pressed it to the wound, wiping the blood from his face with her other hand.

"Natalia, I love you," Trotsky told her. A little later, he said, "Seva must be taken away from all this."

Another guard rushed into the study where Robins was still beating Jacson. "What about *that one?*" Natalia said, referring to Jacson. "They will kill him."

Trotsky's speech was becoming labored. "No, impermissible to kill. He must be forced to talk."

Hansen climbed to the top of the wall and called to the police patrol outside to get an ambulance, then returned to the study. He fought back a sudden impulse to shoot Jacson, the man who had attacked his beloved "Old Man," and joined the other two guards, who were trying to force him to talk about the attack.

Hysterical and in pain from the blows of the guards, Jacson cried out repeatedly, "They made me do it. They have imprisoned my mother." Only the arrival of the ambulance and its police escort put an end to the garish scene.

Hansen rushed back to Trotsky's side, assuring him that everything would be all right.

"No," the Old Man said weakly. He pointed to his heart. "I feel here that this time they have succeeded." He paused for a moment, trying to smile. "Take care of Natalia. She has been with me many, many years."

Hansen and Natalia rode beside him in the ambulance, the tears streaming unashamedly down their faces. They avoided each other's eyes, knowing for certain they were seeing the last of the man they both loved dearly. Trotsky talked to them intermittently as he found the strength, and once he said: "Please say to our friends that I am sure of the victory of the Fourth International. Go forward."

The Fourth International was the organization he had founded and fathered, the Communist group that opposed Stalin as a ruthless dictator, a subverter of the Russian Revolution.

Twenty-six hours and three operations later, Leon Trotsky lay dead in the Green Cross Hospital in Mexico City. All of the skill of the Mexican surgeons and his own almost superhuman fight against death had been unavailing.

The long hours before Trotsky's death were even longer for Frank Jacson. Taken by separate ambulance to the same hospital and placed only a few doors down from the dying man, Jacson's wounds were bandaged and the questioning begun.

"Why?" This was the question asked by everyone—police, newspaper reporters, Trotsky's followers. It was routine police work to uncover the fact that "Frank Jacson" was an alias; it was a different matter to discover who he really was. At first, it appeared he might be a Belgian named Jacques Mornard, but the real Jacques Mornard turned up hale and hearty at home in Belgium. Then who was he and why had he attacked Trotsky?

Before his death, Trotsky had furnished the most likely answer. "He was a political assassin," he had whispered to Hansen in the ambulance. "Jacson was a member of the GPU [Russian secret police] or a fascist. Most likely the GPU."

The court which later tried "Jacson" could be sure of only one thing: that this man had actually killed Trotsky.

The girl Sylvia appeared to be innocent of knowledge about both Jacson and the crime, and she was freed. Jacson himself was tried on a charge of magnicide, the killing of a notable person, and, since the Federal District of Mexico had no death penalty, given twenty years.

During his time in prison, his identity would be established beyond a doubt; once his identity was known, his motives could be reasoned out. But the real story, the story in which "Frank Jacson" was only a bit player, had its roots far back in Russian history. The death of Trotsky, the aging Russian revolutionary, was simply another link in a chain of blood and destruction which had held Russia in bondage for centuries.

★ TWO

"OUR LAND IS GREAT AND ABUNDANT BUT THERE IS NO ORDER in it; come and reign over us."

This was the message sent to the great Scandinavian leader Rurik in 856, by the Scandinavians who had settled around the Lake Ilmen area in what is now northwest Russia. Rurik and his band of fighting men responded and the first Russian state was founded.

The invitation reflected a desire for protection rather than a longing for leadership. The small, weak states, composed of just one city and the land surrounding it, had developed a flourishing trade with the great empires to the south and southwest, a trade that was constantly endangered by the wild tribes which then surrounded them. In addition, the city-states were accustomed to collecting tribute from the farmers who lived in the areas around the town. Occasionally, the farmers rebelled, refusing to pay. A fighting force such as Rurik's could perform a double function, they reasoned. Rurik's men could protect the trade routes and keep them open as well as insure payment from the reluctant farmers. In this way, they would more than pay for the small tax they would collect from the merchants.

Rurik stayed only a few years and accomplished little. His successor, Oleg, proved more ambitious. One of his first moves was to extend the amount of territory under his sway and then to move his capital to Kiev, farther south. Rurik's son, Igor, took over the reins from Oleg and continued his policy of encouraging trade and extending the state, and in the process firmly establishing the house of Rurik as the Russian rulers. From Igor, the throne passed from father to son in an unbroken chain until the death, in 1054, of Yaroslav, the great-great-grandson of Rurik.

Unable to decide upon one of his sons as an heir to the throne, Yaroslav instituted the rota system, a complex plan whereby the nation was broken down into separate territories and each son would be prince of a particular territory. The territories were graded by importance and the eldest son was to have the most important, the second son the next most important, and so on. The plan was even more complicated in its other provisions. When one prince died, all those beneath him would move up one step and the sons and grandsons would also be fitted into the line of succession.

The end result was all too simple, however: by dividing the land, it left it open to attack and conquest by invaders. For a century and a half, the separate princes and their heirs battled with the wild tribes, who were again attacking them.

The trade which had been so profitable in the united Russia began to decline again, bringing hard times in its wake. Serfdom, the condition of semislavery in which the poor of Russia were held for generations, resulted. Peasants, unable to make a living, borrowed from the wealthy families, contracting to work on their estates in payment for the debt. Too, the spasmodic raids from the wild tribes made the big estates, where all could join together and fight in the common defense, safer than the isolated and solitary cottages of the free peasants.

But even while the Russians were battling against want and invasion, other forces which were to have a profound and lasting effect on their future were taking shape in the East.

The Mongols, long dominated by the Chinese, had decided to move north to escape that domination. Once settled in their new home, the tribes quickly fell under the leadership of fierce Genghis Khan. His first move may have been motivated partly by revenge: he led his armies against their former masters, the Chinese, defeating them decisively. From there, he turned his face to the west.

The Mongols, or Tatars, swept through Russia almost at

will, crushing the resistance of the Russian princes. They raided, destroyed, took captives as slaves, and left finally only on orders from Genghis Khan himself. It was not until after his death that the next raids began, led this time by Batu, his grandson. In a matter of a few years, all Russia had fallen under his sway and was paying him tribute.

Tatar domination of Russia lasted almost two and a half centuries. The Tatars did not actually occupy Russia; instead they sent periodic raiding parties to collect tribute from all its inhabitants, plundering and destroying as they went. Gradually the custom was established whereby the prince of each territory collected the tribute from his subjects and delivered it to the Tatar Khan, thus saving his territory from the depredations of the visiting Tatars.

The territory of Moscow, small and unimportant as it was, had been left out of the rota system that Yaroslav had set up. Consequently, with no hopes of succeeding to a better territory on the death of an elder as the other Russian princes did, the princes were forced to extend their territory by purchase, by marriage, or whatever other means came to hand. By 1328, when Ivan I became prince, they had been able to change Moscow into a large and powerful province, despite the Tatars.

The shrewd and ambitious Ivan (who was called Ivan Kalita) actively sought favor with the Tatars by frequent visits, prompt and full payment of tribute, gifts, and other devices. Eventually he was able to persuade the Khan to proclaim him the Grand Prince of All Russia, and each heir who would follow him as Prince of Moscow. The other princes did not like the arrangement but none chose to challenge Tatar power and Russia was once more united under one ruler, although still paying tribute to the Tatars.

It was one of Ivan Kalita's descendants, Ivan III, who finally drove the Tatars out of Russia. The end of Tatar rule did not mean the end of Asian influence, however. Russia has remained since the time of the invasion a peculiar mixture of East and West, both in peoples and in culture. In fact, it has sometimes seemed more East than West. As late as the seventeenth century, some of the tsars were so suspicious of westerners that they carefully washed themselves after being in their presence.

At the time of the expulsion of the Tatars from Russia, the Western world was caught up in the tremendous period of reawakening and invention which has come to be known as the Renaissance, a period which bypassed Russia completely. Russia seemed to be settled in the backwash of history until some of the rulers began to realize that progress depended on closer ties with the West and tried with varying degrees of success to import Western ideas and methods.

Ivan, the victorious warrior, made some efforts in this direction by importing Greeks and Italians to counsel him on many different subjects from diplomacy to architecture. It was Ivan, too, who first adopted the title "Tsar," a title which was passed on to his successor, his grandson Ivan IV, better known as Ivan the Terrible.

Ivan IV was an outstanding example of the worst of the Russian tsars. He made three lasting contributions to Russian history: his almost legendary cruelty, his extension of Russia's borders to the east, and the extinction of his own dynasty or family. In one of the fits of rage for which he was famous, he murdered his own son, leaving as an heir one other son, a halfwit named Fedor who produced no children.

Fedor's brief reign was followed by the "Time of Troubles," an era of upheaval which ended in 1613, when young Michael Romanov, a descendant of the family of Ivan IV's first wife, was elected tsar by an assembly of noblemen and government officials. The Romanovs ruled for more than three hundred years, producing some bad tsars, many mediocre ones, and a few great ones, such as Peter I, Michael's grandson.

Peter came to full power at the age of twenty-two in the last years of the seventeenth century. One of his first moves was to undertake an unprecedented journey to the West, touring nearly all of Europe in his search for ideas and inventions which would help his native land.

During his travels, he studied and examined everything from coffin-making to shipbuilding and returned to Russia determined to persuade the Russian people to adopt the new ideas, by force if need be. He hired hundreds of craftsmen and brought them back to teach their skills to his own people. He even tried to change the personal habits of his countrymen, believing that they were outdated.

In Germany, he ordered complete outfits of Western-style clothing for his magistrates. One of his deputies then called them together and announced:

"I have stringent orders from the Tsar to require you to wear these garments and to remove your beards. Will you obey?"

The deputy paused and looked around at the assembled magistrates in their traditional long, belted gowns and their full beards. There was a muttering of dissent.

"No?" he continued. "Then make yourselves ready for a journey to Siberia."

The magistrates wept, begged, fell on their knees and protested. On a signal from the deputy, soldiers rushed in and began herding them toward the carriages waiting outside. A new bridegroom, perhaps thinking of his bride, was the first to break.

"I remain," he said. "Let the will of Heaven be done."

The other changes made by Peter were equally spectacular and much more important. He simplified the Russian alphabet, eliminating useless symbols and making the letters look more like Latin. He discarded the ancient Russian calendar, which supposedly dated time from the creation of the world, and adopted a modern one. He made far-reaching changes in the government in order for it to work more efficiently and without so much duplication of effort.

Peter created the first Russian navy and built up the army until it was the largest in Europe. And, like many tsars both before and after him, he tightened the bonds on the serfs. In 1722, just three years before his death, Peter issued an edict which forbade the serfs to leave the landowner's estates without written consent. As though to offset that move, he also began the first elementary school system, opened the first hospital and the first medical school.

He left behind him a peculiar and notable monument: the city of St. Petersburg, later called Petrograd. Having acquired territory on the Baltic Sea, he decided that Russia needed a seaport and set about to build it. The land was all swamp and every structure had to be set upon piles driven deep into the ground. It took ten years and the labor of untold millions of serfs. Close to one hundred thousand died of disease and exhaustion during the construction period.

Despite the fact that it was almost impossible to reach from the inland because of the swamps that surrounded it, Peter ordered all government offices moved there in 1714. He also ordered the nobles to build houses there and laid down rules for their size. Afraid of the fires that periodically ravaged Moscow, he commanded that all houses must be of brick or stone and forbade the use of stone anywhere else in Russia until St. Petersburg was complete.

Whatever Peter's personal faults, and historians are agreed that he had many, he was without a doubt the greatest leader Russia had ever produced and he made the biggest imprint on history. The task he set for himself, that of transforming Russia from a medieval to a modern country, was such an overpowering one, it is small wonder that his success was not complete. He did, however, bring Russia into contact with the Western world and set up a governmental system which remained virtually unchanged to the end of the monarchy.

Peter was succeeded by his wife, Catherine I, who held the throne for only two years, then by several descendants, each reigning briefly and without great importance. It was not until thirty-seven years after his death that Russia found itself another leader who was capable of leaving a mark on history.

Catherine II, sometimes called Catherine the Great, ascended to the throne in 1762 as a result of the murder of her husband, Peter III, the grandson of Peter the Great. That Catherine assisted in ousting him from the throne is a fact; that she also had a hand in his murder was accepted by many of her own subjects as true. Catherine was a peculiar mixture, a brilliant woman who was respected and admired by the greatest minds of her day but whose lack of morals made her notorious in a country where debauchery was accepted as standard conduct for the ruling family.

She left many memorials behind her at the end of her thirty-four-year reign. Enlarging upon Peter I's plans, she laid the foundation for a truly national system of elementary education; she built libraries, hospitals, and schools.

Since the beginning of serfdom, mobs of peasants had occasionally attacked the large estates, burning the houses and murdering the occupants, and more rarely, organized and widespread revolts against the government and serfdom occurred. The last of these, Pugachev's Rising, took place during Catherine's reign.

Emilian Pugachev, an illiterate peasant-soldier from southern Russia, was its leader. The uprising began among the Cossacks, but the wily Pugachev, playing on the peasants' superstitions by claiming to be Catherine's dead husband, Peter III, was able to draw large numbers of them into his band of marauders. The group, numbering sometimes as many as thirty thousand, sent a wave of fear throughout the country. Pugachev encouraged his followers to violence and looting, promising to rid Russia of the nobles, take Catherine off the throne and put her in a convent, and enthrone her son Paul.

The army managed to defeat the peasants. They captured Pugachev and took him to Moscow, where he was beheaded. But smoldering fires of resentment still burned throughout the nation. From then on, occasional revolts flared up, ending in the 1917 rebellion, which completely changed Russia's destiny and, perhaps, the world's.

Catherine's greatest contribution to the future of her country was in the amount of territory she added to it. During the period of the French Revolution when the rest of Europe was waiting and watching fearfully the developments within France, Catherine was busy in Turkey and Poland, acquiring more lands. Even when the others took military action against the French republican government, Catherine remained uninvolved, preferring to attend to her own national concerns.

The death in 1796 of Catherine, reigning monarch of Russia, far overshadowed the guillotining of a surveyor named Gracchus Babeuf in Paris that same year. Yet Babeuf's influence on the future of the country Catherine so loved was to be in some ways greater than her own.

Babeuf, an ardent supporter of the French Revolution in the beginning, had finally come to the conclusion that the revolution was not far-reaching enough. He organized a secret society, called the Conspiracy of Equals, and planned to overthrow the government and institute a new kind of society based on communal ownership. The group had done no more than issue pamphlets to persuade others to their way of thinking, when they were betrayed to the authorities and Babeuf was arrested and executed.

The type of society Babeuf envisioned was not really new; it was almost as old as mankind itself. Most primitive tribes were organized on the basis of common ownership of the land. The Greek and Roman philosophers as far back as 500 B.C. had put forth the idea of abolishing private property. In 200 B.C., a Hebrew sect known as the Essenes had actually set up such a society on the banks of the Dead Sea.

The early Christians themselves had believed that it was necessary to give up one's individual title to lands and goods in order to truly follow the teachings of Jesus Christ. But as Christianity spread and members began to be measured by the millions, the early ideas faded and the Church itself functioned as a guardian of the concept of private property. Only a few heretical sects held onto the early beliefs.

The Renaissance, with its emphasis on Greek and Roman thought, had stimulated again the interest in a society in which "each should work according to his capacity and receive according to his needs." The term *socialism* had gradually come into use as a label for these ideas.

Sir Thomas More, a great English scholar of the sixteenth century, had written a book about an ideal society based on socialism, a society which he called "Utopia." Many writers and philosophers took up the idea but it remained in the form of an ideal, something that could be achieved if mankind could be made a little better, a little wiser, a lot less acquisitive. Various groups, mostly religious, had even tried to put the idea into practice.

But Gracchus Babeuf added a new element: the plan to institute such a society by force, by revolution against the existing government. He had organized a secret society and devised a plan by which his ideas could be put into effect, not someday, but then.

Babeuf died in the same year as Catherine the Great, but unlike Catherine, he was unsung and unlamented except by a few faithful followers. But his ideas, which came to be known as Babouvism, lived on, gathering countless converts in the unrest that went hand in glove with the Industrial Revolution then gathering momentum in Western Europe.

The Industrial Revolution, like the Renaissance, had little impact on Russia, where Paul, Catherine's son, now ascended to the throne. Paul was a weak, undisciplined young man whose actions were dictated largely by his hatred of his mother rather than by any desire to aid his country's progress. He firmly believed that she had killed his father and once, finding splinters of glass in his food, accused her of trying to kill him, too, so that she could remain on the throne.

Paul in his turn was strangled by conspirators working with his son Alexander, who later in life was so overcome with guilt that he became a religious fanatic. He developed calluses on his knees from spending hours and even days kneeling on the stone church floors. Visions of his father's mutilated body haunted him the rest of his life.

It was during Alexander's reign that the first truly revolutionary groups were formed. Large numbers of young Russians in military service were stationed in France and Germany during the early 1800s and were there exposed to the ideas of Babeuf and others. Many of them, too, became aware for the first time of how backward, both po-

litically and socially, their own country was, compared to
the rest of Europe. On their return to Russia, they began to
form groups similar to those in the other countries they had
visited.

The ringleader of the movement was Paul Pestel, the son
of a governor general in Siberia, himself a war hero and
aide-de-camp to a Russian army general. Pestel's ideas were
a peculiar hodgepodge of what he had learned abroad and
his own thinking. He believed fervently that the monarchy
must go but wanted a dictatorship by the combined aristoc-
racy and military to take its place. He believed also that
private property should be done away with entirely. Peasants
were to have the use of the land but not the title to it.

The first group founded by Pestel in 1816 was in St.
Petersburg and was named the Union of Salvation. A year
later, the name was changed to the Union of Welfare; four
years later, it was dissolved due to lack of interest when
Colonel Pestel was transferred to southern Russia. This first
group was comparatively mild and had as its goals such
things as constitutional government, economic development
of Russia, and prison reform. It was only later, after Pestel's
transfer, that he was able to organize a group that more
nearly reflected his own thinking. The Northern Society,
the sister organization to Pestel's new Southern Society, was
more moderate. Freedom of speech, press and religion, trial
by jury, freedom for serfs—these were the aims of the Northern wing.

Pestel was not satisfied, however, and continued to work
for the adoption of his own views by both groups. Among his
plans was one for the assassination of all members of the
royal family. This, he felt, was the only way in which Russia
could achieve a more liberal government.

Alexander I, through his secret agents, was kept fully informed of Pestel's plans but made no effort to disband the
groups. He had been a liberal in his younger days and was
still sympathetic to some of their views. He felt also that his
agents who had infiltrated the group would be able to forestall any violent action that the group might undertake.

The announcement of Alexander's death in December, 1825, and the resulting confusion about who was to take the reins of government gave the conspirators their chance. Since Alexander's only child had died years before, the logical successor was Constantine, Alexander's brother, but he had renounced the throne when he married a commoner several years before, in favor of his younger brother, Nicholas. The announcement had never been made public, however, and at Alexander's death, Nicholas was reluctant to step forward without public knowledge of the agreement for fear the people would think he was overthrowing Constantine and so turn against him. So he waited for Constantine to make his position known.

Meantime, the conspirators, led by Pestel, decided that this was a golden opportunity not to be ignored simply because they were not prepared for it. At the very ceremony in which Nicholas would take his oath as tsar, they staged their hastily organized revolt and attempted to stop him. The fight was brief and bloody and ended with the complete defeat of the would-be revolutionaries.

The incident, which came to be known as the Decembrist Revolt, had many repercussions, however. Nicholas exacted a hard revenge. Some of the leaders were exiled to Siberia at hard labor, some jailed, some sent to the mines. The five adjudged the most guilty, including Pestel, were hanged.

That five men should be hanged in a country where the death penalty had been outlawed nearly three quarters of a century before by the Tsarina Elizabeth, shocked the whole nation and created in Nicholas' countrymen as much fear of him as he had developed of them after the revolt. From then on, Nicholas set himself up as the defender of monarchies in not only Russia but also the rest of Europe. Whoever the king, whatever his policies, Nicholas stood ready to protect him, with military force if necessary.

In the revolutions which swept Europe in 1848, Nicholas stood solidly with the royal houses, interfering diplomatically in some instances, sending troops in others.

"Take heed, ye peoples," he warned the revolutionaries,

"and submit, for God is with us." He was convinced that any uprising anywhere was a threat to his own throne. The real threat lay elsewhere.

During the 1840s, in the secret societies in France, a new word had been coined by the revolutionaries to differentiate their philosophy from socialism, which did not go as far and did not necessarily involve revolution. Taking the Latin word *communis* which means common or general, they formed the word "communism." A group of German workers in London, calling themselves the League of the Just, liked the new word and in 1847 changed the name of their society to the Communist League. Later in that year, the League, seeking ways to promote their ideas, approached a bearded, scholarly writer named Karl Marx.

Could he, with his friend Friedrich Engels, write a program for them? they wanted to know. Marx willingly undertook the assignment.

So even while Nicholas was making his famous statement to the European revolutionaries, the first act of the drama which would end with the overthrow of his dynasty, the Romanovs, and the death of every single member of that family, was being played in London, England, a continent away. The printing presses were rolling out a few hundred copies of a slim volume called *The Communist Manifesto*. Written by Marx and Engels, this book was to have echoes through unmeasured time.

★ THREE

THE YOUNG KARL MARX SAT HUNCHED OVER A SMALL GREEN table in a meeting room in Brussels, Belgium, a sheet of paper in front of him, as his close friend Friedrich Engels spoke to their fellow communists about the need for common ideas and doctrines. Suddenly Marx raised his head and leveled his fierce eyes at the young German visitor across the table from him, one of the multitude of nameless revolutionaries who traveled Europe in those days.

"Tell me," he said harshly, ignoring the rest of the assembly, "you who have made so much stir in Germany with your communist propaganda and have won over so many workers that they have thereby lost their work and their bread, with what arguments do you defend your social-revolutionary activity?"

The young man stirred uncomfortably then began explaining that it was not his task to develop new theories but rather to open the eyes of the workers to their terrible situation.

Marx, his thick black eyebrows pulled into a deep scowl, interrupted him. "It is simple fraud," he said sarcastically, "to arouse people without any sound and considered basis for your activity. To go to the workers in Germany without strictly scientific ideas and concrete doctrine would mean an empty and unscrupulous playing with propaganda."

The young man's face reddened and his voice rose with excitement as he tried to defend himself against Marx's charges, explaining how he had organized hundreds of men in the name of brotherly love. It did not matter, he insisted, if they were ignorant of ideas and theories.

Marx leaped from his seat, striking his fist on the table so violently that the lamp danced, shouting, "Ignorance has never helped anybody yet!"

To Karl Marx, even at twenty-eight, it was not enough simply to talk people into revolting against the existing order. They must understand why revolution was not only necessary but inevitable. And even more important, they must know what to do after the revolution to assure themselves of a better world. The task to which he and Friedrich Engels devoted their lives was that of developing the ideas of communism into a system and explaining that system to the world. *The Communist Manifesto* was only one of a mountain of writings produced, both jointly and separately, by the two.

To outward appearances, the two friends were as different as their ideas and beliefs were alike. Karl Marx was the son of a middle class German official. His childhood was an ordinary one by the standards of the day. At the university where he studied law to please his father for whom he had a tremendous admiration, he was known to his fellow students as a workhorse. He belonged to the Poets' Club, fought a duel with a fellow student, became engaged to the girl next door—all activities which were within the pattern of his time and class. But as his education proceeded, he found himself more and more interested in philosophy and less and less in law. To the disappointment of his father, he decided at graduation to stay at the university and get his doctor's degree in philosophy.

Marx hoped for a position as a professor but did not get it, partly because he was known to belong to a group which favored a constitution for Germany. Instead, in 1842, he took a job as editor of a liberal newspaper published in France. When a rival newspaper accused his paper of having communist tendencies, Marx took the accusation seriously and thoughtfully. Knowing little about communism, he decided to read up on it.

He was still reading when he met Friedrich Engels, who had just recently become a communist. No one could have seemed a less likely convert than Engels. The son of a wealthy manufacturer, he had never known a moment's want in his life. He loved music and poetry, had a lively mind and a quick smile. But he had a tender heart for others' problems, too, and the terrible conditions he had seen in Manchester, England, where one of his father's factories was located, had convinced him that drastic action must be taken to change the situation.

The friendship of the tall, fair Engels and the dark-haired, intense Marx was to last a lifetime and result in a complete and systematic communist philosophy. The ideas were to come mainly from Karl Marx; it was Engels' role to add to those ideas and help support Marx so that he might continue in his work.

Marx advanced many new ideas; among them were the economic interpretation of history and the doctrine of class struggle. The most important of these to social thought in general has been the economic interpretation of history.

Until Marx, there had been many attempts by philosophers and historians to explain the course of history. Some tried to interpret history in terms of its heroes, and held to the idea that great men were responsible for changing the way in which the world developed. Others argued that religions were more important because they gave people goals and rules for living that caused them to behave differently, thus changing history. Still others believed that the political side of life, governments and kings, was the most important.

But Marx offered a new explanation. All of these things were important, he said, but the real key to understanding the development of society was the economic relationships of that society. By economic relationships he meant the ways by which people produce, exchange, and distribute the things they consider necessary to living. Whoever owned the means of producing those things would rule society, he believed. Thus in an agricultural society, the landowners would be the ruling class. In his own time, during the Industrial Revolution, it was the owners of the power machinery and the factories who were the real rulers, he said, and they, quite naturally, ruled in their own interests. Therefore, he reasoned, if the people as a whole are to benefit, the people as a whole must own the means of production.

This led to the second point of his philosophy: the doctrine of class struggle. The owners or ruling class, he said, were counterbalanced by the workers or the ruled class. Each was governed by its own needs and desires. Therefore, the ruling class would not voluntarily give up its power but would instead use every means of maintaining it, such as making laws to protect its property and keep the other class down, and so on. Consequently, any change had to come about through class struggle or revolution. Only when there was just one class, the workers or proletariat, would there be no further need for revolution. And, since governments were merely the means by which the rulers kept the ruled in subjection, there would be no need for government and it would wither away.

Marx called his ideas scientific socialism, as opposed to the utopian socialism of former times, which, he scoffed, was based on vague dreams instead of the laws of history. The biggest mistake of these thinkers, he told Engels, was in believing that a few intellectuals in the upper class could bring socialism into being. The truth was that the lower classes would have to fight for it themselves. This was the purpose of *The Communist Manifesto,* to explain some of the ideas and to goad the people into action.

At first the *Manifesto* had very little effect. It was not put on sale and few people other than the members of the Communist League to whom copies were sent even saw it. It was years before an edition appeared in Russia, partly, perhaps, because of Karl Marx's contempt for that country, which he considered too backward to be of interest and without possibilities so far as communism was concerned, and partly because of the tight censorship exercised by Tsar Nicholas I. Despite the wretched conditions, Nicholas held firm to his belief that the discontent of the people was due to ideas coming in from outside and he stopped all travel to other countries except on official business. Through this and other repressive measures, he made himself one of the most hated tsars in history. As famines raged across the land and strikes by factory workers multiplied, even Nicholas had to admit the failure of his program. On his deathbed, in 1855, he said sadly to his son, Alexander II:

"I am not turning the command over to you in good order."

When his death was announced to the palace courtiers, they were so indifferent that they did not even look up from their card game.

Alexander's basic beliefs were not too different from his father's, but the increasing number of peasant uprisings in which manor houses were burned and noblemen murdered with pitchforks convinced him that something must be done. The result was the freeing of the serfs in 1861.

The average ex-serf found himself no better off than he had been; indeed, in many cases, his situation was worse. The land still was not his. The government had bought land from the nobility but instead of selling it outright to the peasants, it had been sold to the mirs or villages. The ex-serf now belonged to the village instead of to a nobleman. He was allotted a certain amount of land to work and out of the proceeds, he had to pay his share of the mir's debt to the government, plus heavy taxes.

Often there was not enough left for him to live on and thousands were forced into the towns, where wages were already at starvation level and workers lived in the most dreadful conditions, sometimes sleeping on the factory floor beside their machines because of the lack of housing and their extreme poverty.

Alexander made further attempts to still the rising tide of discontent by granting some small measure of self-government to the people. For the rural areas, zemstvos or elected assemblies were set up for each county and province; for the cities, a legislative council called the duma was created. In both the zemstvos and the dumas, the nobility and the wealthy had the largest voice, but the assemblies themselves had very little power.

These partial measures were not enough and disappointment over them led to the first organized protest groups in Russia. In St. Petersburg, the capital, university students held demonstrations against the government and Alexander called out his Cossacks, crack cavalry units, to ride them down. Many were imprisoned; hundreds more expelled. "V narod!" ("To the people!") became their rallying cry. Alexander might defeat them, they reasoned, since there were only a few hundred of them. But if they could arouse *all* the people . . .

The Narodniks, as they came to be called, moved out into the rural areas, taking any jobs that were available in an effort to win the peasants' confidence and educate them to the need for overthrowing the regime. The peasants were far more concerned about the land shortage than about the tsar, however, and they gave little attention to the young outsiders and their "big-city" speeches. "Heaven is high and the tsar is far off," the peasants answered and returned to the never-ending stream of chores that must be done if they were to keep from starving to death.

Other reformers moved with missionary zeal into the factory towns and tried to organize meetings at which they read Karl Marx's writings to the workers. They were no more successful than their rural counterparts. Finally, in the 1870s, the government seized their leaders and their printing presses and the movement collapsed.

But the seed had been sown and the plant continued to grow. The would-be revolutionaries had learned a lesson and the next group they formed was better organized. They chose the name "Land and Freedom," designed to appeal to both peasants and factory workers. Committees were set up to spread propaganda, organize strikes and riots, even to assassinate government officials.

Many of the members objected to the killings, however, and the organization soon split into two groups. One aimed at working peacefully and without force to improve conditions; the other, well schooled in the violence and terror by which the tsars had held the people in subjection for centuries, now sought to turn those same methods against the tsar himself.

They called themselves "The People's Will" and Alexander had only contempt for them and their name. It was *God's* will that he was on the throne, he said. What did the People's Will matter in that case? God would protect him from them, he believed. He disdained to take precautions against them; they were not that important.

For a while, it seemed that he might be right. One high official after another fell to the assassins and Alexander escaped almost miraculously. Last-minute changes in plans caused him to miss mined bridges; a bomb in his dining room exploded just before he entered; railroad tracks were blown up shortly after he had passed over them.

The revolutionaries grew more desperate. They held meetings to practice bomb-throwing; they made detailed charts of Alexander's daily routine and of the routes he took to various places about the city. Finally, on a cold, blustery Sunday in March, 1881, they succeeded. Three of them, two men and a woman, were waiting along the street as Alexander passed in an open carriage, escorted by six Cossacks.

When he reached the point directly in front of the first assassin, the woman signaled with her handkerchief. The home-made bomb was seconds late and instead of landing in the carriage, exploded among the Cossacks. The procession stopped and Alexander jumped from the carriage to check on his escort, thanking God that he had not been hurt.

"It is too early to thank God," the second assassin shouted and hurled his bomb at Alexander's feet.

The lower half of the tsar's body was horribly mangled by the explosion. "Back to the palace, quick," he commanded. "Let me die at home!"

It was not until after his death that it became generally known that earlier that same day he had put his seal of approval on a new plan for a national advisory council elected by the people. True, the council would not have the power to make laws or write a constitution, but it was a tremendous step forward toward a voice in government for the Russian people.

Now the country waited to see what his son Alexander III would do with the plan. Would he withdraw it and imply disrespect for his father's last wishes? Or would he put the plan into action, thereby giving the radicals—some of whom had actually murdered his father—at least part of what they wanted?

Alexander settled the question promptly. Just one week after his father's death, he announced that he was against the plan. "I have complete faith in the strength and truth of the autocracy," he said.

He left no doubt about his attitude toward radicals and would-be reformers, either. The leaders of the People's Will were captured and six of them, four men and two women, were hanged. Many others were arrested and lived out their lives in dungeons. Still more escaped or were exiled abroad. Among these was a young man named George Plekhanov.

Plekhanov, the son of a small landowner, had joined the Land and Freedom movement while still in his teens. When the organization had split, he went with those who opposed the use of terror and violence. Russia's problems were overwhelming, he believed, but wholesale murder was not the answer.

Alexander III did not differentiate between those who wanted to change the government by force and those who used peaceful means, however. Staunchly conservative, even reactionary in his views, Alexander had no patience with anyone who disagreed with him.

"There is no government in Russia," he boasted. "There is myself and my servants who execute my orders."

A part of those orders read: Plekhanov and the other liberals and reformers must go, either to prison or out of the country where they could not spread the contagion of their ideas.

In Geneva, Switzerland, George Plekhanov found some of the answers for which he had been searching. Through

Alexander I

Alexander III

Peter I
(the Great)

Alexander II

Ivan
(the Terrible)

Catherine II
(the Great)

Yaroslav
(the Just)

Nicholas I

Nicholas II

Russian Rulers

other exiles, he discovered the writings of the early socialists, of men like Babeuf, and finally, Karl Marx. Here was the key to the new society! The blueprint for action! The mistake of the Land and Freedom group, he came to believe, had been in thinking that Russia could move directly into a socialist state. According to Marx, it would first have to become capitalistic; then it could become communistic. It was the workers in the factories, not the peasants on the farms, who would save the nation. To the idealistic Plekhanov, still in his mid-twenties and filled with missionary fervor, every word was gospel.

A group of exiles soon gathered around him, sharing his enthusiasm for Marxism. Some of them made the journey to London to sit at the feet of the aging Marx and discuss with him the problems posed by Russia's backwardness in comparison to the rest of Europe and America. Their imaginations were fired by tales of the First International Workingmen's Association, a group organized by Marx a few years before to bring together communists from all over Europe in a common cause. Unfortunately they had disbanded in bitterness after an argument between Marx and Michael Bakunin, another Russian refugee.

Back in Geneva again, Plekhanov and the others agreed on the necessity for a new organization based on Marxist principles. In 1883, the same year as Marx's death, they formed the League for the Emancipation of Labor. It was a small group, made up primarily of people like Plekhanov, who began to look and act more like a university professor than a revolutionary. But it would grow, Plekhanov believed. Just how far and how large, not even George Plekhanov would ever have guessed.

★ FOUR

IT WAS A BLEAK, COLD DAY IN EARLY MARCH, 1887, WHEN THE boy, Vladimir Ulyanov, appeared before the schoolteacher in response to her summons. She handed him the letter she had received from a friend in St. Petersburg and watched him silently as he read it. His face showed no emotion at all.

"It's a serious matter," he said finally.

It was indeed a serious matter. Only a year before, the boy's father had died, leaving behind a widow and six children, the eldest, Alexander, a student of great promise in science at the University of St. Petersburg. Now, according to the letter, Alexander had been arrested and was to be tried for having a role in an attempt to assassinate Tsar Alexander III.

There had been no official notification; it was only by chance that the family had learned of the matter at all. But it was true, nonetheless, Madame Ulyanov found when she reached the capital. Sasha, as he was called by the family, was guilty. What kind of times were these that turned quiet, studious young men into would-be assassins? she wondered. Times of unrest and misery, of strikes and uprisings, put down with increasing cruelty by a tsar who would not give an inch to the demands of the people, a tsar so merciless and so autocratic that young men like Sasha Ulyanov saw no hope for the future unless Tsar Alexander III was removed from his throne.

Sasha Ulyanov was hanged two months later. Back in Simbirsk, the Ulyanov family began to learn more of the kind of times these were. Old friends and neighbors avoided them. With the police constantly on the alert, searching out the disloyal, who could afford to be seen with a convicted terrorist's family?

Vladimir, just turned seventeen and about to graduate from the gymnasium, the Russian equivalent of high school, plodded doggedly through his last few weeks, devoting himself to his studies with enough diligence to win a gold medal for being at the top of his class. Then his mother sold their house and furniture and the family moved to Kazan in central Russia.

It took Vladimir only a few months at the University of Kazan to learn that the brother of a revolutionary—even a dead one—carried his past with him. He attended a student protest meeting, watching without speaking, as some of the students criticized the unfair policies of the Minister of Education. The next day he was expelled. When he applied for re-admission, a notation was made on his application identifying him as Sasha's brother and he was refused.

With no job and unable to go to school, Vladimir was bored and restless. There were no goals in his life—nothing to live for. He had lost his religious faith when Sasha died. He filled his time more and more with reading, searching for something to replace that faith. He found it in Karl Marx.

He was not alone. All over Russia students, frustrated by the dreadful conditions within the country and by the absence of any legal ways to work for their betterment, were turning to Marx's writings as the answer. But it was only after his mother had persuaded the Minister of Education to let him take his final examination in law and he was working for an attorney in St. Petersburg that Vladimir made contact with others like himself.

It was there, too, that he first heard the magic names, George Plekhanov and the Emancipation of Labor. Vladimir threw himself into the work of the secret groups; he could not learn enough. In a short while, he was organizing groups and distributing Marxist propaganda. It was a short step from there to writing pamphlets himself. It was obvious by then that Vladimir had found a faith to hold to, and his blind and ruthless devotion to it marked him even then as a leader of the future, a man who was to gain power and use it, a power as great as that held by Alexander III.

Alexander had used that power only to repress, however, not to build, and his death in 1894 left his son Nicholas II with the same set of problems that Alexander himself had inherited, grown worse through having been ignored for thirteen years. And, unhappily for Russia, Nicholas was even less capable of coping with them than his father had been. Alexander had never put too much faith in intelligence; character was more important, he had insisted. He had been particularly proud of his own great physical strength, sometimes tying an iron poker into a knot to astound his guests. But even he had misgivings about the abilities of his son. Once when a government official suggested that Nicholas might preside over a particular ceremony, Alexander replied, "Don't tell me you haven't noticed that my son is a complete nitwit."

Nicholas seemed to have some doubts himself. "What am I to do?" he wailed after his father's death to one of his cousins. "I don't even know how to talk to ministers."

Weak-willed and disliking responsibility, the twenty-six-year-old Nicholas nevertheless found himself crowned tsar of all Russia, a country where unrest was growing daily. Alix, his young German bride, was of a sterner nature although no more capable than he of holding the reins of state.

"Make people feel who is boss," she advised him. "Put ministers in their place; speak angrily, raise your voice to them, even shout."

Nicholas tried. When liberals approached him shortly after the death of his father about instituting a government of law in Russia, he called their ideas "senseless dreams."

"I have sworn to them . . ." he said, referring to the people, "to preserve the autocracy unabridged and to hand it intact to my son. I will not break my oath."

So government by whim continued and discontent built toward the inevitable explosion. Because of the increase in population, the size of the average farm plot had shrunk while taxes had increased tremendously, leaving the peasants worse off than ever. Often they could not pay the taxes and tax collectors sometimes flogged whole villages in an attempt to wring money from them, money they literally did not have.

In the cities, strikes, although illegal, were frequent and costly. Russia's industry was growing during the first few years of Nicholas' reign, primarily because of the large amounts of foreign capital being invested there. Prices were rising fast and wages were not keeping pace so that the factory workers suffered from poverty almost as great as the rural peasants. In addition, the long hours and lack of all safety precautions and sanitary measures meant that death, injury and disease were the daily companions of the workers.

As unrest increased, so did the activities of the revolutionaries. The young Marxist Vladimir Ulyanov was busier than ever writing and distributing pamphlets on communism and attempting to organize workers into secret groups, so busy that in the spring of 1895, he fell ill of pneumonia. His recovery was slow, complicated by stomach trouble, and he took the opportunity to apply for a passport to Switzerland for "medical treatment." The time had come to meet Plekhanov, the exiled leader of Russian socialism.

It was a meeting of fire and water. Ulyanov found "the Old Man" cold and distant, content to talk of revolution in abstract terms, as though it were a hundred years away.

Plekhanov had long recognized his own shortcomings as a revolutionary leader. He knew himself to be too much the intellectual, too refined in his tastes and outlook. This red-bearded young man, though, this Vladimir Ulyanov— Plekhanov sensed the driving force within him, the aggressive intelligence which could be translated into action. Here, Plekhanov felt, was the future leader of Russian communism. Here was the man who would accomplish what the others talked of.

Ulyanov returned to Russia in the fall, more dedicated than ever to his ideas. With two friends, Nadezhda Krupskaya and Julius Martov, he produced a flood of Marxist literature and helped to foment a wave of strikes in St. Petersburg. He and Martov began a new organization whose militant purpose was obvious in its title: the Fighting Union for Liberation of the Working Class. They were successful in leading many of the old study groups into joining the new organization; they laid plans for a secretly published newspaper which would serve as a voice for the movement and a link between the small, scattered groups.

On the eve of their first edition, the police, who had been following Ulyanov since his visit to Plekhanov in Switzerland, decided to close in. He, Martov, and several others were arrested and held in St. Petersburg prison. He had planned well, however. Before his arrest, he had taught his fellow conspirators a code by which they might communicate and also a technique for writing between the lines of a letter in milk which would turn brown when heated. Through such devices, he was able to keep his position as leader of the St. Petersburg group and direct its activities during his year in prison and his three years of exile in Siberia.

Martov also spent three years in Siberia but widely separated from Ulyanov. The delicate-looking but daring Krupskaya escaped the first series of arrests only to be caught in a later police dragnet and sent into exile. Describing herself as Ulyanov's fiancée, she asked to be sent to the same place as he, and surprisingly, her request was granted. They were married shortly after her arrival.

Ulyanov continued to send back secretly coded and smuggled programs for a plan he and Martov had been working on at the time of their arrest—a plan for a meeting of the scattered study groups throughout Russia to form a single, all-Russian social democratic party. Finally, in 1898, his hopes and plans materialized.

A handful of delegates from a variety of organizations met in Minsk in western Russia and formed the Russian Social Democratic Labor Party. Spied on constantly by the police, the delegates left hurriedly after only three days, without writing a constitution or a program. They planned to do these things at another meeting, six months in the future. The police took steps to see that they did not; nearly all of the delegates were arrested almost immediately after disbanding. But the organization, once breathed to life, could not be killed that easily; others kept it going and the small, relatively unimportant meeting at Minsk came to be known in later years as the First Congress of the Russian Communist Party from which all subsequent congresses are numbered.

Ulyanov was one of the few who recognized the importance of the Minsk meeting. He recognized, too, the new party's need for leadership and discipline. He threw himself with renewed vigor into his reading and writing. His whole personality seemed to change during the last few months in exile. His laughter was seldom heard again; his temper shortened and he lost weight. He began having difficulty sleeping and often he sat up all night making plans for the revolution he was certain was coming. In January, 1900, when his term of exile expired, he walked out, not as the ardent, emotional, young Vladimir Ulyanov but as the ruthless, relentless, almost legendary Lenin.

No one knew why he chose the name "Lenin" or where it came from. Some said it was the name of a guard in Siberia whose passport Vladimir Ulyanov used; others said he took it from the Lena River, which runs through Siberia. He had used pseudonyms before, some of them many times, but this time—when he wanted to leave Russia illegally and get to Plekhanov in Switzerland—he chose a new one and it stuck to him for the rest of his life. Sometimes he signed "N. Lenin," usually just "Lenin" and that was the name by which the world was to know him.

Leaving Krupskaya to finish her term in exile, Lenin arranged to meet Martov, who had been released at the same time. Together they made their way with forged passports across the Russian border and into Switzerland. Plekhanov had a place for them; he and a few others were drawing up plans for a newspaper to be called *Iskra (The Spark)*, which would be published in Germany. Lenin and Martov would both be useful on the editorial board; Lenin, since he had already won recognition as a writer on communist theory and doctrine, would be a major contributor to the paper.

It was the kind of work Lenin liked best and he put all his driving force behind it. More and more, through sheer energy and will, he tended to overshadow Plekhanov, to take over the duties and decisions that were by right the older man's. Occasionally they argued over policy but Lenin usually won even before the fight began.

"Plekhanov is like a greyhound who bites and lets go," one of their coworkers said. "Lenin is like a bulldog who bites and doesn't let go."

Iskra was an immediate success. Copies were distributed to Russian exiles in Europe and even smuggled into Russia itself, where it was looked upon as the official voice of the Communist Party. Lenin was now completely disillusioned with Plekhanov because of his caution and his professorial ways. When it became necessary to leave Germany to continue publication of *Iskra,* Lenin took an open stand against him. Plekhanov wanted to move back to Geneva; Lenin held out for London. In 1902, the paper and Lenin, along with Krupskaya who had then been released from her Siberian exile, moved to London.

It was here, in their London apartment, that he and Krupskaya were awakened in the middle of the night by a loud knocking at the door. For a revolutionary, an unexpected caller was always a threat. Was it the police—or secret agents from Russia? They waited until it sounded again, then relaxed. It was a code knock, the sign that a fellow conspirator was outside. Krupskaya opened the door, and a young man burst through it and into Lenin's bedroom. Lenin, sitting up in the bed, was at first overwhelmed by the flood of words that poured from him. Then he smiled and sent Krupskaya to pay the cab driver who still waited outside the door. It was "Pero"—the Pen—the young revolutionary whose writings, smuggled out from his exile in Siberia, had already brought him fame in communist circles. Now he had escaped and had come to join the movement.

Krupskaya returned to find them engaged in earnest conversation, like two old friends. Although this was their first meeting, each was acquainted with the other's writings. And each recognized the other as his kind of revolutionary: steel-hard, dedicated and determined. Lenin and Leon Trotsky—"Pero"—sealed a friendship that night which, with few interruptions, would last a lifetime.

They had come to this moment by vastly different routes. Leon Trotsky, born Lev Bronstein, came not from the comfortable middle class like Lenin, but from peasants; his family were among those uncounted millions whose lot it was to wrest their living from the land by never-ending toil. His people were a little better off than most and he had never known real privation, but neither had he ever known leisure or luxury.

Trotsky had spent a year at the village school, then back to the farm and its morning-to-night round of chores, a routine that was disrupted a short while later by the arrival of his cousin, who had been expelled from the university and had been sent to visit in the country for a time. The young man amused himself by tutoring young Trotsky, teaching him not only academic subjects, but something of manners and culture as well. When he returned home to Odessa and married, it was arranged with the boy's father, who, though illiterate himself, placed a very high value on education, that young Trotsky should live with the couple in Odessa in order to complete his schooling.

Odessa was then a hotbed of radicalism and it was inevitable that he would make contact with it. It was inevitable, too, that with the kind of quick, agile mind he had, he would be intrigued by it. He began attending secret meetings during his last year in the gymnasium or high school. He listened and he learned. At first he disliked Marxism, mostly because it was too systematic, but by the end of his first year at the university, he had embraced it completely and had joined in the activities of the secret groups. He helped organize a South Russian Workers Union, wrote and distributed pamphlets, even began a newspaper.

In January, 1898, he had been arrested. Two years in prison, two more years in exile in Siberia, then the opportunity had come to escape. By now firmly committed to revolution and Marxism, he made his way straight to the headquarters of *Iskra,* which he had seen during his exile.

Plekhanov did not have the same reaction to him that Lenin did, and it was only after an argument between the two that Trotsky succeeded in getting a job with the paper. Lenin wanted him on the editorial board but Plekhanov held firm and he was put to work writing articles and helping to raise funds by lecturing to various groups, mostly political refugees from Russia itself.

The stories told by the refugees were encouraging. Increased discontent caused by the depression which had struck at the turn of the century was bringing more and more people into the Marxist movement. New organizations were being formed throughout Russia, many of them affiliated with the Russian Social Democratic Labor Party, as the communists called themselves, but some, such as the Social Revolutionaries, as independent groups.

The S.R.s, as they were known, based their organization on a combination of Marxist ideas and terrorism. Their specialty was assassination of public officials and robbery of banks and government agencies. In the tremendous wave of unrest that was sweeping through Russia, they were finding a wide scope for their activities. Strikes and uprisings began first with the factory workers, as in St. Petersburg, involving as many as thirty thousand workers, and spread to the peasants. In 1902 alone, the police had to put down more than three hundred peasant uprisings. Manor houses were burned, timber and grain seized, landowners callously murdered by starving peasants. The methods used by the police became more desperate as the violence increased. In at least one instance, at Poltava, police officials flogged an entire village, guilty and innocent alike, into insensibility in an attempt to stop the disorder.

There was no doubt about it; Russia was seething with revolution. But it was as yet without direction or leadership.

Tsarist officials searched feverishly for schemes with which to calm the citizenry. Labor unions, although illegal, were mushrooming all over the country and were a potential source of trouble. In an effort to combat their influence and direct their protests away from the Tsar, organizers in the secret pay of the police were sent out to form rival unions.

Who was to lead the people? Not Nicholas, certainly. He and Alix refused to trouble themselves unduly with affairs of state; that was the concern of the officials he had appointed. In his diary, Nicholas kept careful account of the walks they took, the picnics, the games they played, the progress of their four young daughters, but seldom mentioned the government or his duties as tsar.

Lenin, Trotsky, Plekhanov, and Martov—the leaders of the Russian Social Democratic Labor Party—were equally busy with their own affairs. A second Party Congress had finally been arranged and convened in July, 1903, in Brussels, Belgium.

The trouble between Lenin and Plekhanov, on the surface a difference of opinion on various matters, but actually a fight over who was to be the leader of the party, broke into the open at the Brussels meeting. There in the deadly summer heat of an abandoned flour warehouse festooned with red bunting in a pathetic attempt at gaiety, Lenin made his bid for power by suggesting many changes in basic policy.

But it was Martov, not Plekhanov, who accepted his challenge. Martov, his friend from St. Petersburg, the man with whom he had stood trial and been imprisoned and exiled, led the opposition on each point Lenin raised. Party membership must be restricted to the active workers, Lenin said. No, Martov answered, it must be open to all. On each point that Lenin raised, Martov was the spokesman for the other side.

At the suggestion of the Brussels police, whose spies were making meetings difficult, the congress adjourned to London and the fight continued. Surprisingly, Plekhanov took Lenin's side in many of the arguments. And even more surprisingly, his friend Trotsky stood with Martov. In the end, however, Lenin won. His proposals received the majority support from the congress and his followers came to be called Bolsheviks, which means majority men; Martov's were known as Mensheviks or minority men.

Lenin returned to Geneva, where the editorial offices of *Iskra* had been moved. He was exhausted but triumphant, for he had won every single important fight. The editorial board of *Iskra,* which in actuality was the leadership of the party, was now to be cut to three instead of six and he was one of the three. The trouble with Martov and Trotsky had led to an open break and Plekhanov was on his side.

However, Plekhanov was now entertaining second thoughts and was not sure whose side he was on. He did not like Lenin's manner and thought he acted too much like a dictator. Martov and the Mensheviks had proposed a more democratic program and organization. So Plekhanov approached Lenin about a compromise between the two factions.

But the die was cast. Lenin had made his bid for power and now he must stand or fall with it. He promptly resigned as editor of *Iskra* and he and Krupskaya left for an extended vacation.

There were others like him, he found on his return, enough of them so that another newspaper could be started, this time without interference from Plekhanov and Martov and without sharing his authority with anyone. His time was coming, that much he knew. When or how, he was not yet sure. In Russia, the government had become involved in a war with Japan that was unpopular with the people. The unrest continued and grew. The opportunity would come; it *must* come.

★ FIVE

THE BITTERLY COLD JANUARY WIND SWIRLED THE SNOW AROUND the hem of Father George Gapon's long robe as he led the procession through the streets of St. Petersburg, holding the beautiful Russian Orthodox cross reverently in front of him. Behind him, people eddied out of every side street to join the mass that was swelling into a flowing river of humanity, headed toward the Tsar's Winter Palace. As they marched, they sang "God Save the Tsar."

Who would have dreamed a year ago that he would be here now, at the head of two hundred thousand men, women, and children, going directly to the Tsar himself to present a petition? Only a year ago, in 1904, with the secret cooperation of the St. Petersburg police, he had formed the labor union called the Assembly of Russian Factory and Mill Workers. It had grown fantastically. Within the year, it had reached a membership of nine thousand but many thousands more attended the meetings and participated in the activities.

It was good, Father Gapon thought, to keep the workers out of harmful, political activities and to direct them toward worthwhile recreation. That had been his purpose from the beginning. Many socialists had joined his group; many of his members had become socialists. But that was irrelevant, really. The aims of the organization were still the same; to keep workers contented with their lot and out of trouble and to provide recreation. Some of the socialists spoke from time to time but the workers were not really interested.

What they wanted was to bring their woes to the attention of Tsar Nicholas II. They were convinced that the terrible conditions in the cities, the slums, the low wages, the long hours, were the fault of others, not of the Tsar, who loved his people and wished them well. When the members had first talked to Father Gapon about writing a petition and presenting it directly to the Tsar, the young priest had been against it. But after thinking it over, he was uncertain. Perhaps the Tsar could do something about the dreadful poverty and want in which his people existed. So finally, he had allowed himself to be convinced; later he had become enthusiastic about the project. The date had been set; word had gone out to the workers. Committees had been formed to make sure that no hot-heads joined the procession and caused trouble for them all. The committees searched each person who joined the procession for weapons and took away the few they found so that they were in fact what Father Gapon's letter to the Tsar the day before had said they would be: loyal, peaceful citizens on the way to receive the blessings—and perhaps, if God granted it, the help—of their temporal father, Tsar Nicholas II.

But Father Gapon, like his flock, had misjudged Nicholas. Always weak and easily frightened, Father Gapon's letter had panicked him completely and, instead of waiting inside the palace to appear on the balcony above them as they expected, Nicholas was miles away in the country, safely hidden along with Alix and their children. He had left a reception for them, though. Cossacks and other troops were posted along their route and massed in the square in front of the Winter Palace. And they had been left with orders to stop the march and turn back the marchers.

But the crowd was ignorant of all this and they paraded happily toward their destination, bearing huge pictures of Nicholas on posters and interspersing patriotic songs with hymns. It was not until the first lines reached the bridge that provided access to the Winter Palace that they became aware that all was not as it should be.

There they were met by police, who demanded that they disperse. The front lines slowed but those in back, now blocks long, could not hear or see what was going on and continued to march forward. Father Gapon and the others in the lead protested that they were a peaceable group, come for an audience with the Tsar. The forward thrust of the thousands behind them kept them moving forward, regardless of their own desires.

Once again the police yelled to them. "Disperse! Back!" The crowd kept moving onward.

"Stand back!" shouted the officers. "Back or we shoot!"

The inexorable tide of people kept moving. "Fire!" shrieked a frightened voice from the police side.

All along the way, police and troops opened fire on the unarmed families. Cossacks, armed with long flails or whips, began riding through the seething mass, striking out indiscriminately. Hundreds fell and the crisp cold air was rent with screams from the injured and the dying. There was a kind of hysteria about the scene now as the soldiers and police kept shooting into the crowd. Father Gapon had fallen or stumbled and lay silent now in the hard-packed snow.

When it was over at last, there were more dead and wounded than could be counted. They lay all along the way, in the streets, in front of famous Kazan Cathedral, in the square of the Winter Palace. The bloodstains on the white background of snow stretched literally for several city blocks. Newspaper reporters at the scene gave the dead and wounded at 4,600. Men, women and children had died together in the streets of St. Petersburg because Tsar Nicholas II had been afraid of them. Unarmed, singing hymns, carrying pictures of him, they had been shot down like mad dogs. Never again would anyone in Russia believe that the Tsar loved his people and wanted the best for them. Now he was lumped with all the other villains in their lives—the landlords, the factory owners, the bureaucrats. They had lost nearly five thousand lives, but Nicholas had lost the loyalty of the common people, the ones who had stood by him so firmly until now.

Father Gapon was physically unhurt when he picked himself up from the snow. But his heart was changed; it was sick with the thought that he had been in some way responsible for this massacre that would be known for all time as "Bloody Sunday." There was one idea uppermost in his mind: to get away, to escape all this. He was a fugitive now, a man whose past loyalties had been torn violently from him. As soon as he could, he fled, making his way finally to Geneva and Lenin.

Lenin heard of "Bloody Sunday" the next morning. He and his wife went to a little restaurant, a favorite for Russian refugees. There they joined in the singing of a revolutionary funeral march for their fallen countrymen. Afterward, Lenin threw himself feverishly into reading and translating books on revolutionary techniques. How to organize, how to make weapons, how best to fight—these were the things that Lenin needed to know, he felt. He was convinced that the revolution in Russia had begun and that history had chosen him to play a role in it. He must be ready; he must have the knowledge when his moment came.

Leon Trotsky heard the news that morning, too. But it was not Trotsky's way to wait. Still quite young, overpoweringly impetuous, he left for Russia that day. He and the other communists must make sure that the revolution succeeded. And more than that—that the communists had control of it.

News of the bloody massacre filtered slowly through Russia itself. Everywhere men heard about it and new disturbances started. Workers went out on strike; peasants rose up and began a renewed attack on landlords, burning and killing. Four hundred thousand struck during the month of January alone. By February, Nicholas knew that something must be done. This time the people were determined to have some relief from the burdens they carried.

In desperation, he agreed to the calling of a National Duma or legislature. It was not to have the power to pass laws, however; its purpose was to consult with the Tsar and offer him advice. To Nicholas, who believed totally in the absolute power of the monarch, the proposal seemed like a big concession to make.

The people took a different view. A few years before, perhaps even a few months before, Nicholas's proposal would have been enough to satisfy them. But not now. Now they were insisting on a constitution, on civil rights, on universal suffrage, and an end to the war with Japan.

Even the intellectuals and the professional people joined in the protest movement. Doctors, teachers, lawyers formed unions and joined together in a Union of Unions. There were rumblings of mutiny in the armed forces.

Abroad, the communists took heart from the situation. But the Bolsheviks and the Mensheviks called conventions to discuss what might be done, the Bolsheviks in London, the Mensheviks in Geneva. Lenin found time to meet with Father Gapon and hear the story firsthand.

The Father had presented himself first to George Plekhanov, the founder of Russian communism, but Plekhanov, always antireligious, had dismissed him gruffly. "No good can come of a priest," he said.

Lenin disagreed. The Bolsheviks could use a priest just as readily as anyone else. After talking with Father Gapon, Lenin began a fund-raising campaign among sympathizers in Europe, giving the proceeds to the priest for arms, to be bought in London through contacts of Lenin's and delivered to the strikers inside Russia. But again Father Gapon's efforts were doomed to failure. He purchased the arms and hired a ship to transport them, only to have it sink in a storm in the Baltic Sea.

Inside Russia, conditions steadily worsened. Unrest seemed to sweep through the services like an epidemic. In June, the sailors aboard the *Potemkin,* the newest and most powerful battleship in the Black Sea fleet, threw their officers overboard, hoisted a red flag and turned their guns on the town of Odessa, sailing then to Rumania, where they appealed for political refuge. On another Russian ship where a similar revolt occurred, sixty crew men were shot or sent off to penal servitude.

Delegates from the zemstvos or provincial legislatures, fearful for the future, begged the Tsar to call the Duma he had promised, hoping that would satisfy at least some of the people. Taking several weeks to reply, the government finally announced its decision. The Duma would be called but elections for it would be indirect, that is, the people would vote for others who, in turn, would vote for delegates to the Duma. Also, there would be high property qualifications for voting so that the common people would not be able to vote at all.

Again, it was too little and too late. The uprisings began with renewed vigor.

A new round of strikes began when the bakers and printers in Moscow walked out. Within a few days, workers in St. Petersburg struck in sympathy with them. A short time later, the illegal Railroad Union in Moscow went out on a strike which spread like a prairie fire throughout Russia. Within days all transportation and telegraph service was halted. Strikers were demanding an eight-hour day, full civil rights and a constitutional convention.

It was almost as though a national holiday had been called. Each hour new groups joined the strikers. Small shops closed their doors; schools, banks, public utilities companies, government offices—all of them locked up and their employees joined the milling crowds in the streets. Even the ballerinas in the national theater walked out. In the streets, mobs of people sang the "Marseillaise," the song which had been born in the French Revolution more than a century before and had since become the theme for all revolutionists everywhere.

But it was not a holiday. With stores closed and the railroads idle, food could not be transported and sold and hunger or even starvation became an immediate problem. Fuel became desperately short. The whole nation was paralyzed, with some cities cut off from all outside contact. In a few places, strikers set up barricades in the street and fought armed troops with sticks and stones.

In St. Petersburg, the capital, some of the labor groups in the city decided to form a Soviet (the Russian word for council or committee) to coordinate activities. They began with just forty representatives, but within a month the number had grown to five hundred. The St. Petersburg Soviet began publication of a newspaper, *Izvestia,* which they used to present demands to the City Duma and to the police and to inform the general public of their activities. They elected an executive board and officers to lead them. As vice-chairman, they selected a young man who had been working diligently to spread the revolution, to keep it going, to turn it from a spontaneous expression of the people's discontent into a genuine socialist uprising. The young man was Leon Trotsky, using the alias Yanovsky.

The strike continued to spread. Soviets were organized in nearly all cities. Doctors and lawyers joined the movement. Servants, cab drivers, and postmen walked out. In the provinces, peasants further accelerated their campaign of burning manor houses, seizing crops and murdering landlords.

The government had been forced to conclude a treaty with Japan, ending the war, and now the returning soldiers, miserable in defeat and chafing under the harsh army discipline, began riots of their own. Some units shot their officers and walked out to join the restless mobs. Sailors aboard several ships mutinied.

Everywhere there was total chaos. The government sent troops against the peasants and the workers but there were too many of them and not enough loyal troops. In Sevastopol the ships that had mutinied were bombarded from fortresses within the city and those of the crew that had not been killed in the bombardment or drowned were slaughtered as they reached shore. And still the riots continued.

Thoroughly frightened, Nicholas could not understand what was happening. Didn't the people understand that he had taken an oath not to change the government or its policies? Why were they behaving like this? In desperation, he turned to his chief minister for advice. What should he do?

"Either grant a constitution or restore order by establishing a military dictatorship," he was told. Grant a constitution? But that was against everything he believed in. He approached his uncle, the Grand Duke, about assuming the office of military dictator. The Grand Duke, a realist, threatened to shoot himself on the spot.

So there was nothing left to do but give in to the radicals, Nicholas decided, only so far—certainly not all the way. "You remember those January days after 'Bloody Sunday' . . . they were miserable, weren't they?" he wrote to his mother. "But they are nothing in comparison to what has happened now. It makes me sick."

With those feelings, Tsar Nicholas II signed the October Manifesto, promising freedom of speech, press, association and conscience to all Russian citizens. Vaguely he promised universal suffrage, the right to vote, and guaranteed that no law would be passed without the consent of the National Duma, a legislature to be elected by the people.

The recently organized party of Constitutional Democrats, or Cadets as they had come to be called, welcomed the Manifesto; but the St. Petersburg Soviet, through its spokesman, Vice-Chairman Leon Trotsky, renounced it.

"Freedom of assembly is granted but the assemblies are surrounded by the military. Freedom of speech is granted but the censorship exists even as before. Freedom of knowledge is granted but the universities are occupied by troops. Inviolability of person is granted but the prisons are overflowing . . ." Trotsky wrote. "Everything is given—nothing is given." The executive board of the St. Petersburg Soviet, under Trotsky's leadership, voted to continue the strikes.

But the workers had had enough of hunger and cold and unemployment. Wanting to believe that the Tsar would really give them what he had promised, that the fight was over, they went back to work. There was nothing for the Soviet to do but call off the strike officially.

The forces that had been called into play could not be made to disappear quite so easily, however. The radicals seemed to have won their goals, but in winning they had created an opposing force—the reactionaries, those who did not want change of any kind, those who had benefited more from the way Russia had been.

Almost overnight extreme counterrevolutionary groups known as the Black Hundreds sprang up. They operated with the full knowledge—and sometimes the financial backing—of the police to stamp out revolutionary sentiment or ideas wherever they saw or imagined it.

Armed groups were organized, transported to other areas where their members would not be recognized, and given police protection in their acts of assault, pillage, rape and murder. Their marching song was "God Save the Tsar" and they carried religious statues and pictures along with pictures of Nicholas as they committed their acts of terrorism. Printed pamphlets were distributed to the ignorant and superstitious peasants, who were told to make three copies and give them to other villagers. If they did not, the peasants were told, they would be stricken with disease and affliction within six days, and if they did, they would be granted recovery from an incurable disease should they contract one.

The police themselves began a quiet campaign to regain control. Expeditionary forces were sent into the provinces with instructions to punish the peasants and burn their huts. Troops marched in and lined up the villagers, shooting the leaders and flogging the rest. In St. Petersburg, the entire Soviet was arrested and thrown into jail, including Leon Trotsky. A new Soviet was quickly elected to replace them. In city after city, the reactionaries made armed excursions into districts populated by religious minorities and massacred and mutilated hundreds, blaming them for the uprisings.

The Soviet called a second general strike for the middle of November, demanding an end to martial law, and despite the number of Socialists in their ranks, the members rejected a proposal that they join the Social Democratic Party. The members walked out on the appointed day but this time they found themselves alone. The other groups—the professionals, the storekeepers, the government employees—refused to join them, believing that the October Manifesto would solve their problems without further demonstrations.

In three days, the Soviet called off the strike and the workers returned to their jobs once more.

The revolutionaries in Europe had followed events closely and in October when the first general strikes began, Lenin himself had set out for Russia, believing that his moment in history had come. But mishap after mishap occurred to delay him and it was December before he finally reached Moscow. And it was from the Moscow Soviet, where Lenin and other Bolsheviks were in control and the workers were not so exhausted and had not suffered so much, that the third strike call came.

The other Soviets, including St. Petersburg, ignored it. And in Moscow, it began peacefully. A few barricades were set up in the streets by workers singing happily and making jokes. The police did not look upon it so lightly, however, and on the third day, the workers were sobered by a few bloody clashes with police-directed troops. Barricades began to go up in earnest. In response, more troops were shipped into Moscow, armed with artillery and machine guns.

The workers fought with iron bars, clubs, knives, and the few revolvers they had been able to collect, about two hundred altogether against ten thousand fully armed troops. The barricades were of little value except in slowing cavalry charges through the streets. Fighting was from house to house, from rooftops, from doorways and windows, the kind that Lenin had studied so diligently earlier in the year.

"Be merciless," government troops were ordered by their commanders; "take no prisoners." Artillery was set up on the outskirts of the workingmen's district and the whole area was bombarded. Factories, houses, stores—everything was destroyed. Men, women and children suffered and died alike. In some instances, wounded were dragged from ambulances by savage troops and murdered.

Three days—and hundreds of deaths—later, it was all over. It had been doomed from the start; the workers without weapons, without a plan of action, had had no chance of winning against the well-armed and trained government troops. It did not matter whether or not they won, Lenin had said. It mattered only that the masses were prodded into revolt. They had revolted; many among them had died. And now the strike was over. The year 1905—the year of revolution—was over.

The jails were filled with prisoners; the Tsar's promises still hung in the air, unfulfilled. The people were exhausted and numb. With the Moscow uprising, the 1905 revolution had burned itself out. But the fire was not dead. The embers—the strong undercurrent of discontent—still glowed.

The next strong breeze would cause them to burst into flames again.

SIX

NICHOLAS WAS DETERMINED TO REGAIN CONTROL OF THE GOVernment, whatever the cost in human life. Between Bloody Sunday in January, 1905, and the calling of the first Duma, or legislature, in March, 1906, one thousand were executed, twenty thousand wounded, fourteen thousand slaughtered, and seventy thousand arrested.

One of the seventy thousand was Leon Trotsky, the leader of the St. Petersburg Soviet.

His sentence was exile to Siberia. He had expected it; there was no surprise on his face, only a renewed determination. He had escaped it once; he could do it again.

As the train carrying him and other political enemies of the government proceeded eastward, the guards grew more relaxed and cheerful. After all, there were no towns in this part of the country, only a few isolated peasants' cottages. Any man foolish enough to attempt an escape could be easily tracked through the snow and ice and recaptured if he survived the elements long enough.

To Trotsky, it was worth the chance. At one of the infrequent stops, he approached the guard.

"I feel ill," he said, touching a hand to his forehead. "Is it all right to step outside for a breath of air?"

The guard shrugged carelessly. Where could a lone man go in the Arctic Circle without arms or equipment?

Trotsky stepped down from the train and walked casually around the station. Once out of sight, he wasted no time. Using the persuasive powers that had brought him fame as chairman of the St. Petersburg Soviet, he talked a peasant into driving him 430 miles in a deersleigh to a settlement.

From there, by horseback part of the time, on foot and by train, he made his way to Finland and freedom.

Father George Gapon, who had led the march on the Winter Palace which had ended in Bloody Sunday, chose a different course. Disillusioned and bitter, he returned to Russia from Europe. The revolutionaries had gone too far, he felt. Reform? Yes. But not the complete overthrow of everything, the Tsar, the government, the whole Russian way of life. Better to keep things as they were than that. Again, he went to work secretly for the police.

A few weeks later, his body was found hanging from the rafters of a small, rural cottage.

"It was the police," the peasants whispered in terror. "Will they stop at nothing? A man of God, murdered by the Tsar!"

Only years later did the truth emerge. Father Gapon, like many others, was a victim of the Social Revolutionaries, who had learned of his police connection.

Lenin, too, was gone. Like Father Gapon, he was bitter and disillusioned, but for a different reason.

"Empty promises!" he said angrily. "That's all Nicholas has given. The Duma is a farce." Calling upon the Bolsheviks to boycott the elections, he made his way to Stockholm, Sweden, and safety.

Nicholas was unconcerned. Now that the revolution was under control and its leaders gone from the country, there was no need to fulfill the promises he had made. The people would have their Duma but its power would be strictly limited. In the first place, it would be elected indirectly; that is, the people would vote for electors who would meet and elect the delegates to the Duma. Secondly, there would be another legislative body, a State Council, which would be appointed by the Tsar and the nobility and any laws proposed by the Duma would have to pass the State Council also. And Nicholas would have an absolute veto over any law that might pass both houses. The form would be observed, the people would have their Duma, and Nicholas would have firm control over everything that it did.

Still it was better than nothing, the people said. It was a beginning. The newly legalized political parties campaigned vigorously, all except the Bolsheviks, most of whom obeyed Lenin's orders to ignore the proceedings.

From the first, the meetings were stormy and disorderly. Delegates shouted each other down for a chance to speak; the conservatives and the liberals argued vehemently over every issue. The assembly passed petition after petition demanding the release of political prisoners, universal suffrage and direct elections, without effect. But when they began calling loudly for land reform—measures by the government to provide more land for the poverty-stricken peasants—Nicholas, afraid of getting the peasants stirred up again, sent troops to surround the palace where the Duma was meeting and to disband the delegates.

That taken care of, Nicholas could turn his attention to affairs at home. Through a succession of four lovely daughters, he and Alix had prayed for a son to be heir to the throne. In 1904, their prayers were answered and the tsarevich was born. But it seemed doubtful the child would survive to rule Russia someday, even if the autocracy lasted. He was a hemophiliac, a bleeder. The slightest accident, even a minor bruise or scrape on the shin, could start an attack which could be fatal. The best physicians in Russia, in all Europe, had difficulty stopping the bleeding once it started.

Nicholas and Alix sought frantically for help. The whole court knew of their distress.

"There is a monk," one of the ladies-in-waiting told Alix, "only recently come from Siberia, a miracle worker. Perhaps he could help the young tsarevich."

"How could he help?" Alix asked.

"Who knows?" the woman answered. "He is different. His ideas are different. He has done some strange and wonderful things which cannot be explained."

"What do you mean, his ideas are different?" Alix persisted.

The woman leaned closer. "Gregory Rasputin says that

the closest you can get to God is when you are genuinely contrite or repentant. He says you must sin fully, then you will be truly sorry, and in that spirit you will be close to God."

Alix drew back a little, staring at the woman in disbelief.

"It is true," the woman insisted. "I have seen it myself. After one of his sessions of sinning, there is a holy look about him, a saintly look. I tell you, he can work miracles. He is very close to God."

It was worth remembering, Alix decided. She would find out more about him.

He had covered his tracks well and there was little to discover by casual inquiry. Gregory Rasputin was a type of monk common to tsarist Russia, a wanderer who lived off the bounty of the simple peasants for whom he practiced faith healing and worked what seemed to them to be miracles. He had become a monk rather late in life, at thirty-six, after a checkered career which included a prison term for horse theft and flogging for drunkenness and licentious behavior. His peculiar philosophy about sin had brought him many followers at Court, despite his coarse manners and uncouth appearance.

When the young tsarevich began bleeding uncontrollably again, Alix remembered the episode at Court. "Rasputin," she said to Nicholas, "send for the monk Rasputin."

Nicholas looked startled—a monk? Hurriedly, she told him of the conversation with the lady-in-waiting. "It is worth a try," she finished tearfully.

Rasputin was found and a courier hustled the monk through the corridors of the palace, straight to the bedroom of the tsarevich. Ignoring Nicholas and Alix, the monk sat down beside the deathly pale child and began talking in a low voice. For some time, for hours it seemed to the distraught parents, he sat talking, spinning tales of frontier life in Siberia. Finally he stood up.

"The bleeding has stopped," he announced.

Nicholas and Alix looked for themselves; the doctors were brought in to examine the patient. It was true. Rasputin h somehow stopped the bleeding. Some of the doctors later came to believe that he accomplished this by hypnosis but despite their intense dislike of the evil monk who broke all his religious vows not once but repeatedly, they were forced to admit that he could and did stop the attacks.

In the corridor outside the bedroom, Alix grasped his hands in gratitude. He stared down at her, his dark, fanatical eyes burning into hers.

"The destiny, not only of the child but of the whole Romanov dynasty, is irrevocably linked with my own life," he told her.

Alix gazed back at him in worshipful awe. She had prayed for a savior and he had been sent. She nodded dumbly. Whatever he said was true, she believed every word of it.

Nicholas believed him, too, although he did not fall so completely under his sway. There were other problems facing Nicholas. There was the demand for a second Duma; there was the manifesto issued by the disbanded Duma delegates.

Instead of retiring gracefully to their homes after the dismissal of the Duma, as Nicholas had supposed they would do, a group of two hundred of the delegates had fled across the border to Vyborg, Finland, and there published a statement that had come to be known as the Vyborg Manifesto. In it, they again demanded the rights they had argued for in the Duma itself and they called on the people to refuse to pay taxes until the Tsar allowed the Duma to reconvene.

The people of Russia had become accustomed to more direct action. Riots and mutinies flared in several provinces, and as the government moved to put them down with signers of the manifesto were sentenced to prison, making them ineligible for re-election had a criminal record. This done, a second

ment efforts to ensure a majority of con-ere outnumbered three to one by liberals. met the following spring, the two sides session of debating and name-calling.

Across the continent in London, an almost identical scene was taking place. The Russian Social Democratic Labor Party was holding yet another conference in a vain attempt to heal the split between the Bolsheviks and the Mensheviks. Here, too, the arguments went on and on with no agreements reached. On the surface, it was an argument about doctrine; in actuality, it was a struggle for power with the younger, more determined Lenin challenging George Plekhanov, the founder of the party, for the leadership.

The people in the audience were quiet, containing their reactions within themselves. There was Trotsky, who had chosen to go with the Mensheviks before and now felt the split to be less important. Martov, the man who had spoken for Plekhanov in 1903. Zinoviev, who would run near the heights of power before he was chopped down. Kamenev, a faithful worker who followed Lenin's orders explicitly. And the swarthy, pockmarked Djugashvili, who would be known to the world as Joseph Stalin.

Joseph Djugashvili, or Soso, his nickname as a boy, was born in 1879 in Georgia, a southern province of Russia, a modest two-room house. Poverty and disease were far visitors to the peasant Djugashvili family; three son from them in childhood and the senior Djugashvil succumbed when Soso was eleven, leaving the widowed mother to struggle on alone. Mrs. D tensely religious, encouraged Soso to enter and, by way of preparing him for it, saw tended the village elementary school.

Upon graduation, Soso was able to w the Tiflis Theological Seminary. He h long, however, when he began to chafe u tary discipline. Several years before, M sprung up among the discontented stude himself drawn to them, excited by the id At nineteen, he was expelled from schoo ing Karl Marx's ideas in earnest. He, lik and many others before him, was convinc lay the answers to Russia's problems and joined the revolutionaries who met secretly at Tiflis.

He narrowly escaped arrest in 1901, during a general roundup of Social Democrats, only to fall into the police net a short time later. Upon his release, he moved to Batum, a town in southern Russia, where he joined yet another Social Democratic underground group.

When the chairman of the Batum party was mysteriously denounced to the police and arrested, many party members believed that Soso Djugashvili was guilty. He had already gained a reputation for slandering and intriguing against other party members who held higher positions than his own. There were plans to accuse him openly and subject him to a trial when the police saved his comrades the trouble. He was arrested, held in prison for a year and a half, then exiled to eastern Siberia.

He escaped just over a month later and reappeared again in Tiflis, where he rejoined both the revolutionaries and the young bride he had married during his term in prison at Batum. Unlike the wives of Soso's comrades, Ekaterina was not a Social Democrat. A simple peasant, with strong religious feelings, she spent the time while he was away in ardent prayer that he would turn from his activities and return to God and a quiet life of work and happiness. She bore him one son, then died.

Joseph Djugashvili followed the procession to the cemetery, the pallor of his hard face the only sign of his grief. Pointing to her coffin, he said to a boyhood friend standing near:

"This creature softened my stony heart. She is dead and th her have died my last warm feelings for all human ngs."

t seemed to be true. He threw himself into his revolu ary activities with even more ruthlessness. He met Lenin he first time and was disappointed because this man he evered from afar seemed so ordinary up close. Neverthe e remained a Bolshevik, becoming involved in the bank robberies the Bolsheviks were staging to gain funds for their work. And in 1907, he sat silently in the London hall while Lenin argued from the dais for control of the party. When the showdown came, Djugashvili, or Stalin, as he chose to be called, was among the majority who favored Lenin for Chairman of the Central Committee, the executive board of the party, over the frock-coated Plekhanov.

But Lenin's success did not bring peace with it. During the next few years as he and Krupskaya wandered across the face of Europe, he suffered increasingly from headaches, insomnia and periods of despair and depression.

On New Year's Day, 1912, he told his sister, "I do not know whether I shall live to see the next rising of the tide."

Nor did the other revolutionaries fare much better. Zinoviev, Kamenev and Stalin were all arrested and exiled to Siberia by Nicholas; all three eventually escaped but Stalin was retaken and again exiled. Only Trotsky was able to keep both his spirits and his freedom. While the others continued to devote their time to promoting revolution and publishing the newspaper *Pravda*, Trotsky traveled around the world as a correspondent for various publications.

Behind these small events, even larger ones were looming. Throughout Europe, there was talk of war. Austria-Hungary was interested in the small countries in the Balkan Mountain area; so was Russia. Tension grew as the whole world watched the deterioration of relations between Franz Joseph, Emperor of Austria-Hungary, and Nicholas II, Tsar of All Russia.

"War between Austria and Russia would be very useful to the cause of revolution in Western Europe," Lenin told friend in 1913, "but it is hard to believe that Franz Josep and Nicholas will grant us this pleasure."

Even Rasputin, the evil monk who still ministered to young tsarevich and had become Alix's constant compan was concerned. "Let Papa Nicholas not plan war," he the royal family. "With war will come the end of R and yourselves and you will lose to the last man."

The third Duma, even more ineffectual than the first two, was too preoccupied with its daily rounds of futile bickering to note the gathering clouds of war.

Then on August 1, 1914, despite Rasputin's warning and the conditions within Russia, Nicholas led his country into the almost global conflagration which was to be known in history as World War I.

Russia was singularly unprepared for war. Its industry was not sufficiently developed to support a large military machine. Its armies were ill equipped, poorly trained and badly led. Its government had no plans for mobilizing the country to fight a war.

Lenin was gleeful over the chain of events. "Now they'll see," he said. "War is no accident and no 'sin' as the Christian reverends think. They, like all opportunists, preach patriotism, humanitarianism and pacifism. War is an inevitable part of capitalism."

"It is our chance," he went on. "We must change it from a war between countries to a war between the owners and the workers."

He could scarcely believe it when the reports reached him from other European countries; in each, the Social Democrats chose to break with the party and support their homelands. Even Plekhanov had turned traitor to the cause in Lenin's view and was advocating support of the Allied cause, of which Russia was a part. Lenin, with Krupskaya, retired in disgust to Switzerland to wait out the war.

Inside Russia, the situation grew steadily worse. The country had always suffered a labor shortage and now, with twenty-five per cent of the adult males of working age drafted into the army in the first year and a half of the war, the shortage became critical. Prisoners of war, refugees, women and children were all put to work, but it was not enough.

The creation of a large army also placed a drain on the food supply, particularly since the amount of land in production dropped as a result of the labor shortage. Railway transportation, none too efficient at best, began breaking down, making it doubly difficult to ship what food there was to the parts of the country where it was needed. Hunger became a constant companion to millions of Russians.

It was only one of many problems to the armies. In the spring of 1915, the Germans opened a drive which pushed the surprised Russians, under the command of Nicholas' uncle, the Grand Duke Nicholas, back in confusion. The western provinces and a large part of the rail network were quickly lost along with large supplies of artillery and ammunition. From then on, the Germans could advance without fear of heavy return fire. The severe shortage of arms and ammunition sent waves of infantrymen into battle without rifles, hoping to arm themselves with weapons from their fellow soldiers who were shot down in front of them. Morale, of course, ebbed rapidly.

It fell even lower with Nicholas' announcement that he personally would assume command of the armies. Alix, jealous of the Grand Duke's popularity with the soldiers, had encouraged Nicholas to take the command away from him. She had developed an intense dislike for the Grand Duke because of his aversion to Rasputin.

"I have absolutely no faith in the Grand Duke," she wrote her husband, Nicholas. "I know him to be far from clever, and having gone against a man of God, his work cannot be blessed or his advice good."

For herself, she had no doubts at all of the saintliness of Rasputin, despite the reports of his immoral behavior and his ignorance of political affairs. Time and again, the weak-willed Nicholas was persuaded by her to dismiss government officials and appoint new ones as a result of Rasputin's whims. At first, the uncouth monk had been only a religious adviser to her; later he began to direct not only her whole life but, through her, the affairs of state as well.

His influence was even greater, once Nicholas left for the front. For his part, Nicholas seemed all too happy to turn the reins of state over to Alix and relinquish his role as Tsar. "Dear wife," he wrote her, "don't you think you should help your husband while he is away? It rests with you to keep peace and harmony among the ministers—thereby you do a great service to me and to our country."

Alix was sincere and enthusiastic but not too capable. With Rasputin as her constant adviser, she adjourned the Duma and removed all those who dared oppose any pronouncement either of them made. Her appointees were selected on the basis of their approval of Rasputin. Among them was an ultraconservative landowner named Protopopov, who became Minister of the Interior.

Alix was deaf to all criticisms of herself or Rasputin. "Do listen to him who only wants your good and whom God has given more insight, wisdom and enlightenment than all the military put together," she wrote Nicholas. "His love for you and Russia is so intense and God has sent him to be your help and guide."

More and more, military decisions were made by Rasputin; campaign plans were brought to him to be blessed. There seemed to be no end to his influence.

But there were some who had the courage to oppose him. When he sent word to the Grand Duke that he was coming to the front to bless the armies, the Grand Duke sent him a telegram in reply: "IF YOU COME TO GENERAL HEADQUARTERS, I WILL HAVE YOU HANGED LIKE A DOG."

Rasputin was unpopular with the people, too. Rumors spread like wildfire through the country that he was a paid German agent; some even said that Alix herself was pro-German.

Meanwhile, the Germans pushed steadily ahead, forcing the armies back before them. "This is not war; it is slaughter," one Russian soldier commented. And indeed it was. Casualties numbered in the hundreds of thousands and into the millions before it ended. Many of the soldiers played sick to escape the massacres which the battles actually were. Thousands deserted; more thousands surrendered.

As the German armies advanced, the civilians in front of them fled eastward in panic. What food and supplies the refugees did not trample, the army high command deliberately destroyed to prevent its falling into German hands.

The food shortage now became critical. Electric power-houses and waterworks had ceased to operate in many cities. In October of 1916, the Moscow political police chief reported, "Privation is so great that many people are actually starving." Strikes were increasing ominously.

In St. Petersburg, the Duma reconvened and again attempted to deal with the existing situation. Charges of corruption against high government officials were made and various financial scandals were brought to light.

It was obvious now to everyone but Alix and Nicholas that things could not go on much longer in the same fashion. Innumerable warnings were given them, by the President of the Duma, members of the State Council and the provincial legislatures, even the royal family itself.

"Strange as it may seem," one of them wrote, "it is the government itself which is preparing the revolution."

And toward the end of December, 1916, came another warning, an even more terrifying one. Rasputin's body was found in the river. Investigation proved that the murder had been committed not by the radicals or revolutionaries but by members of the nobility, one a close relative of the Tsar himself! The monk had been poisoned, shot, clubbed, then shot again. His tenacious hold on life had been finally loosened only by the river; the autopsy showed the cause of death to have been drowning.

Instead of coming to her senses as the murderers had hoped she would with Rasputin gone, Alix became even more irrational. Both she and Protopopov seemed to cross the thin borderline of sanity altogether. They began holding seances in which they tried to contact the spirit of the dead Rasputin for his advice on government affairs.

Government in Russia had shrunk to a shadow and that shadow was being felt throughout the land. Soldiers were deserting in droves and carrying back tales of being sent into battle without arms and of the fantastic toll in lives the war was taking. There were rumblings among the peasants—forerunners of an even more deadly round of uprisings. In the cities, each day saw the number of strikes swell to greater proportions as the workers walked out in protest against hunger, privation and the government itself.

In January, 1917, the police report to Nicholas read, in part, "The exasperation of the people is growing by leaps and bounds. Every day more and more of them demand, 'Either give us food or stop the war.'"

In February, the Duma at last reconvened. As one of its first actions, it resolved not to be dismissed again. From the floor, Alexander Kerensky, a representative of the moderate Labor Party, demanded that the Tsar be removed to save the country. In reply, Alix demanded that Kerensky be hanged.

In Switzerland, Lenin was in a mood of hopeless despair. The Russian revolution, which could be the beginning of a global uprising that would end with a communist world, now seemed to him only a dream. Leon Trotsky, working as a war correspondent, was removed from and seemingly unaware of the events in his homeland.

The police report on the army read: "The soldiers began to demand peace a long time ago, but never was this done so openly and with such force as now. The officers not infrequently refuse to lead their units against the enemy, because they are afraid of being killed by their own men."

In March, signs began to appear in the bakeries of St. Petersburg: "No bread today. None expected."

Housewives, unable to buy even the small ration of food to which they were accustomed, clustered in crowds around the locked stores.

On March 8, they were joined by workers. Twenty-four hours later, a total of two hundred thousand were milling in the streets. Troops of the St. Petersburg garrison were called out against them. Three days later, most of them had joined the mob, sharing their weapons with them.

Alix sent word to Nicholas: "Youngsters and girls are running around shouting that they have no bread. They do this just to create some excitement."

The President of the Duma, Rodzianko, wired the Tsar: "THE SITUATION IS SERIOUS. THE CAPITAL IS IN A STATE OF

ANARCHY. THE GOVERNMENT IS PARALYZED. TROOPS ARE FIR-
ING AT EACH OTHER."

"Stop this disorder at once!" Nicholas ordered.

One more day. The strikes had spread like an airborne
disease to the rest of Russia. Rodzianko again wired Nicholas. "THE SITUATION IS GROWING WORSE. THE LAST HOUR HAS
STRUCK, WHEN THE FATE OF THE FATHERLAND AND THE DY-
NASTY IS BEING DECIDED."

Nicholas wired an answer. "DISSOLVE THE DUMA!"

The Duma refused; instead they demanded that the Tsar
abdicate and appoint a responsible minister in his place.
Even Alix, who had spent her married life telling him to be
more autocratic, wired him, ". . . CONCESSIONS ARE NECES-
SARY."

Nicholas replied by telegraph that he was well, it was
lovely weather, and he was leaving for St. Petersburg "to
make the necessary arrangements."

Rodzianko answered, "IT IS TOO LATE." The entire country was in the grip of the revolution.

The St. Petersburg Soviet, or committee of representatives from the various labor groups, which had been born
during the 1905 uprisings, was now hastily reorganized and
added its voice to the general clamor. It was joined by regiment after regiment of deserting soldiers.

On March 15, a few miles from St. Petersburg, near the
town of Pskov, the imperial train was pulled to a siding.
Nicholas Romanov II, in the presence of two members of
the Duma, abdicated in favor of his brother, the Grand
Duke Michael.

The St. Petersburg Soviet announced: "No more Romanovs! We want a republic!"

The Grand Duke Michael refused to accept the crown,
throwing his support to a Provisional Committee which had
been formed by the Duma.

The Romanovs, who had ruled Russia for more than three
hundred years, would rule no longer. The autocracy was
ended.

But what was to take its place?

★ SEVEN

NICHOLAS ROMANOV, EX-TSAR, SAT STIFFLY ERECT AS THE train sped through the Russian countryside. His mouth was twisted into something between a smile and a grimace; but despite that, there was a kind of dignity about him, a quality he had not had before.

There was little dignity in the guards who swarmed over the rest of the train as it covered the miles to Tsarskoye Selo and the imperial palace, near Petrograd, the new name for St. Petersburg. The train stopped at each station and the guards alighted to talk excitedly with their counterparts on the platforms.

"Yes, that man in the front car is Nicholas Romanov!" they shouted excitedly.

"The Tsar himself?"

"The Tsar himself! We're taking him back. He's through, finished!"

"Long live the revolution!" they shouted to each other.

When the train finally reached its destination, Nicholas climbed carefully down and walked calmly to the car which awaited him. Beside him sat one of his attendants, the only one still there. The others had dispersed like leaves before an autumn wind. At the palace gate, he saluted absently, out of habit, returning a greeting that had not been given.

Alix was waiting when he entered the palace. Seemingly cool and self-possessed, she was nervous with fears for the future. They rushed into each other's arms, their eyes filled with tears of humiliation and bewilderment.

"If the whole of Russia now entreated me on bended knee to resume the crown, I would not do it," he said at last.

She pressed his hand in response, then turned and stared at the guards, who stood looking on indifferently. Was this to be their fate, she wondered. Were they always to be captives, prisoners in their own land? She read the answer in the hard faces of the guards. Yes. Yes, they were. And what would happen to the country without them?

The answer came from a surprising source. The Duma, weak and ineffectual until now, displayed unexpected strength. Meeting immediately, they formed a Provisional Government and elected George Lvov, a mild-mannered and well-liked Cadet, President, and Alexander Kerensky Minister of Justice.

"All political prisoners are pardoned as of now," Lvov announced. "As soon as possible, we will pass laws guaranteeing freedom of speech, press and assembly, with no restrictions on individual freedom because of race, class or creed. There will be universal suffrage and a secret ballot. And," he added, "there will be elections soon for a national assembly to write a constitution for Russia."

His statement was applauded by the democracies around the world. Even the Petrograd Soviet gave its support to the program. In the general confusion, the Soviet had taken over many governmental functions, going so far as to establish a militia of workers to replace the police who had either been shot or driven into hiding during the recent revolution. But there was one part of the new government's program they would not support. The Provisional Government insisted that Russia must fulfill its obligations to its Allies; the Soviet called for an immediate end to the war.

In an attempt to undermine the war effort and win the soldiers to its point of view, the Soviet issued what came to be called Order Number One.

"Soldiers are to have the right to elect delegates to the Soviet and to organize committees to maintain discipline in their ranks and punish rudeness to the men by officers. Saluting is hereby outlawed. No troops are to carry out any order that has not been approved by the Soviet."

The pamphlets containing Order Number One were passed from hand to hand in growing excitement.

"The Soviet is behind us now," the soldiers whispered to each other. "Tonight at eight, we will meet in the barracks and elect our representative."

"Maybe we will oust the officers, too, and elect our own," another said, half-jokingly.

"Why not?" one asked seriously.

Many of them did just that. In addition, they refused to obey orders until they had discussed them and taken a vote. Discipline melted away. The demoralization of the army was nearly complete.

Other problems beset the new government. Its officers were besieged by telegrams from cities and villages all over Russia to send competent officials to replace the bureaucracy, which had fled during the revolution.

In mid-April, the problems were multiplied a hundredfold with the return of the exiles. The law passed by the new government giving amnesty or pardon to political prisoners and exiles brought them back by the thousands.

From every corner of the globe they came. Every boat that docked at a Russian port, every train that stopped in a Russian station disgorged its load of returning exiles. Twenty thousand sleighs were needed to bring the ex-prisoners from northern Siberia alone!

Plekhanov came from Europe. Trotsky departed from New York. From Siberia in the mass exodus came Kamenev and Stalin. And from Zürich, Switzerland, came Lenin.

From the moment he had news of the revolution, he had been wild to return to Russia. All kinds of impractical schemes —even the idea of an airplane to carry him over the front lines—had been conceived, investigated and discarded. The final solution was the most fantastic of all.

The German government—Russia's enemy in the war— agreed to his traveling through Germany, through the fighting zone, into Russia in a sealed railway car. They guaranteed his safety in the hope that his presence in Russia would hurt the Russian war effort.

On April 16, 1917, mobs of people thronged the platform, spilling over into the waiting room of the Petrograd depot known as the Finland Station. A bell clanged in the distance; then a few minutes later, the brightly lighted train pulled up in front of the crowd. The door was thrown open and through it walked Lenin.

At the first sight of him, a roar went up from the crowd. Workingmen near him hoisted him to their shoulders and carried him into the imperial waiting room, the room formerly set aside for the Tsar and his family. The mob followed, its red banners of welcome held high.

"Speech! Speech!" they shouted.

The lines of weariness in his face seemed to fade as he looked out at them. He could see the awe reflected in their expressions. Here was the legendary Lenin, they seemed to be saying, the man of iron who believed in the revolution so completely that he had lived as an exile all his adult life. Strength flowed back into him as he stood there; his voice seemed to explode over them.

"Unite against the Provisional Government," he cried to them. "Put an end to the imperialist butchery! Stop the war!"

Again the masses roared their approval. Forming a ring around him, they escorted him into the square outside. Bands played the old revolutionary songs; the crowd shouted his name over and over like an incantation. Searchlights weaved across the square, calling attention to the forest of gold-lettered red banners. He stopped beside the armored car that was to whisk him to Bolshevik headquarters.

"Long live the world-wide socialist revolution!" he called to them.

"Long live the world-wide socialist revolution!" they echoed.

He had waited a long time for this moment. He stood there, savoring it a little longer, rocking back and forth on his heels, a small smile curling his lips, then climbed into the car.

The return of the exiles had a profound effect on the Petrograd Soviet also. It had been liberal before; now, under the influence of Lenin and others like him, it became radical. It continued to call for an end to the war and at the same time added a new demand: more power in the government must be given to the Soviet, the true voice of the people. The Soviet leaders and members became more openly contemptuous of the Provisional Government and its lack of control over the country.

"It will never amount to anything," Lenin sneered.

Alexander Kerensky, who had lately taken on the job of Minister of War, tended to agree with him. "The government is already nonexistent," he said despairingly. "It does not work but merely discusses its condition."

What had happened? Why was the Provisional Government now floundering after having made such a courageous beginning? First, its members could not agree among themselves about the solutions to the overwhelming problems Russia was facing. Secondly, they were getting little support from the people themselves.

There was no doubt that the people had been profoundly affected by the sudden ending of governmental restrictions. At first, they seemed to have an unlimited sense of freedom; they were like children on a holiday. They had thrown the Tsar out; there was no government. They were free, free to do whatever they liked! That mood had been followed by a feeling of shock, of terrible weariness. The war and then the revolution had left them exhausted. Factory workers quit work; soldiers at the front quit fighting; peasants left their plows standing in the fields. They began to resent the new government with its laws and attempts to restore order. The Soviets seemed to be different. They, too, wanted an end to the war; they had something definite to offer. More and more frequently in the cities, huge signs were displayed. "More power to the Soviets!"

Lenin agreed. "The Provisional Government is capitalist in sympathy," he argued. "Power must be transferred to the Soviets, the truly revolutionary form of government. We must end the war! Then we will nationalize farm lands. Production and distribution will be controlled by the Soviets."

And, he added privately, the Bolsheviks must win control of the Soviets. Now, he said, "The Soviets will be the government. We must be the Soviets."

As the spring and summer progressed, more and more Soviet members were being won to his point of view. The other groups—among them the Mensheviks and the Social Revolutionaries—were falling apart, splitting between the Soviets and the Provisional Government. Leon Trotsky, formerly a leading Menshevik, drew closer to Lenin and adopted many of his ideas. Meetings of the Petrograd Soviet were loud, long and quarrelsome as the different factions struggled for control.

"We must unite!" George Plekhanov, the founder of the party, urged at one of the meetings. "We must not divide our strength!"

Led by the Bolsheviks, the crowd booed and hissed until Plekhanov retreated from the platform, angry and discouraged.

"Instead of a revolutionary, you are now a counterrevolutionary, according to your own party," a friend said as he walked away.

"If those maniacs are revolutionaries, then I am proud to be called a reactionary," Plekhanov answered heatedly.

"Have a care," the other man cautioned, "lest you be arrested as soon as these people, your own pupils, become dictators."

But despite their problems in the party, the Bolsheviks continued to win increasing support from the people, largely because of their stand against the war and because of the new slogan they had adopted. "Peace, land, bread and power!" promised something for everyone. Then the Provisional Government made an almost fatal mistake.

Yielding to the demands of their Allies for a second front to relieve some of the German pressure in France, the Provisional Government ordered a military offensive against the German army on the west. Neither Lvov, the President, nor

Kerensky, the Minister of War, seemed to realize how sick of war the people and the army were.

For a few days, the offensive went well and the Russians advanced slowly but steadily; but then the Germans were reinforced and began counterattacking. The result was disastrous. Order Number One, three years of war, and the Bolshevik peace propaganda had done their work. The totally demoralized army took to its heels and fled, leaving only remnants behind.

Reinforcements were badly needed and the rumor spread quickly through Petrograd that troops stationed there were to be sent to the front. Meetings were hastily scheduled.

"The government is sending us to be slaughtered!" one of the soldiers told the meeting.

"It was the Tsar's war. Why should we give our lives for a meaningless war begun by the Tsar, who is no longer our ruler?" another asked.

"But what can we do?" many voices called out.

"The Soviet! The Soviet is against the war; they will help us. We will show the government we will not fight."

"If the government will not stop the war, we will stop the government!"

"That's it! We will show our sentiments and our strength!" A whole chorus joined in now. That was the answer: the Soviets would help them organize. Delegates were sent to seek the help of the Soviet in an armed demonstration against the government and the war.

The Soviet refused. Then what about the Bolsheviks? The delegates sought out Lenin and Trotsky, who had now become Lenin's closest ally. They listened carefully, then talked it over.

"Do we have the strength to overthrow the Provisional Government now? That's the question," Trotsky said.

"Perhaps," Lenin answered, "but do we have the strength to stay in power once we have seized it?" He sat thinking for a moment, then shook his head. "No," he said. "Not yet."

The delegates returned to their barracks. "No one will help

us," they reported to their fellow soldiers and sailors. "Whatever we do, we must do alone."

Without leadership, without organization, as though by magic, soldiers, sailors and workers filled the streets of Petrograd the next morning. The day before, the city had been ominously empty; now it echoed to cries of "Down with the Provisional Government!" "All power to the Soviet!" Government troops and rebels clashed bloodily in several districts throughout the city. Night fell and with it, a blanket of calm descended over the city. Was this to be the end of it?

With the morning came a renewal of the restlessness. Soldiers and sailors from nearby bases swarmed into Petrograd. Crowds of them appeared at the headquarters of the Bolsheviks. They stood outside, chanting "Lenin! Lenin!" until he appeared on the balcony.

He spoke to them listlessly, offering little encouragement. The time still had not come for him, he believed. Later in the day, it seemed that he was right. Reports began coming in that the government was succeeding in checking the rebellion, the streets were clearing. Kerensky, who had been making a tour of the front to try to raise morale, was on his way back.

The situation looked bad to Lenin. It was common knowledge that he had refused to play a role in the uprising because he was gathering up his forces to make his own bid for power. Sooner or later, the Provisional Government would have to get rid of him and the other Bolsheviks to protect itself. The riots could be used as an excuse.

"Now they will shoot us down one by one," he told Trotsky. "This is the right time for them, before we become stronger."

But the shots were paper instead of lead. A government-inspired newspaper story charged Lenin with being a German agent, backing the story up with the fact that the Germans had engineered his return to Russia.

"So that's why he wouldn't help us!" the troops exclaimed to each other as they read the story. The story seemed reasonable; they believed it. More meetings were held and the decision was made to throw their support to the Provisional Government. The Bolshevik following faded away. Without fear of a military uprising, Kerensky now ordered the arrest of the Bolsheviks.

Once again Lenin was a hunted man. Wearing a borrowed raincoat and a cap pulled down over his eyes, he slunk through the streets, on the move constantly. A few nights later, he boarded a westbound freight train and found refuge with friendly peasants some distance away. Zinoviev joined him and the two of them spent their time writing, talking and reading the newspapers. There had been many stories of his escape, he discovered (one of them had him leaving Russia in a German submarine), but there was one thing they had in common. In all the papers, to the public at large, he was known as "the traitor, Lenin." The lines in his face deepened; the stress of the situation began to tell on him in many ways but he remained convinced that his time was coming. He had a place in history and he was fast approaching that place.

In Petrograd, the discouraged Prince Lvov gave up and submitted his resignation as president of the Provisional Government. The logical choice, the only man in the government who appeared to have the courage to act was Alexander Kerensky, the brilliant, flamboyant, young Minister of War.

But Kerensky was not equal to the job that must be done. He found himself torn both ways at once. The conservatives in the government did not approve of the "democratic" way things were going, particularly in the army, and urged him to make some changes. The liberals were also dissatisfied and threatening further trouble.

To satisfy the conservatives, he finally agreed to appoint General Lavr Kornilov as Commander-in-Chief of the Russian Armies. Kornilov, who had won his commission under the Tsar and was widely reputed to have "the heart of a lion and the brain of a lamb," promptly dissolved the soldiers' committees and announced in Petrograd that the Soviet should be disbanded and all Bolsheviks hanged. The leftists responded with immediate cries for his dismissal.

Meanwhile, the Germans were marching steadily toward Petrograd, Lenin had escaped to Finland, and Trotsky was still imprisoned, having been taken in the roundup following the July rising. Kerensky, fearing for the safety of the royal family in such a turbulent situation, had them moved to western Siberia.

Then there was a new problem to face.

"There are stories," an aide told him, "that General Kornilov is going to attempt to overthrow the government and set himself up as dictator."

"But where would he get support?" Kerensky asked incredulously.

"They say it is from the industrialists and landowners, the conservatives," the aide answered.

Kerensky paced the floor. "I have never trusted him," he said bitterly. "It was a mistake to appoint him. See what you can find out."

The answer came quickly. "It's true," the aide reported back. "Even now he is massing troops for a march on Petrograd. He tells them it must be saved from the Germans and the Bolsheviks."

Kerensky thought for a moment, his head in his hands, an expression of despair on his face. "We need all the help we can get," he said finally. "Order the release of the Bolsheviks from prison; write up a formal request to the Soviet for aid in defending Petrograd from Kornilov—and from the Germans," he added.

With the returned Bolsheviks, the Soviet formed a Committee to Fight Counterrevolution. The Red Guard, a military force twenty-five thousand strong and armed with machine guns and rifles, had been organized by the Bolsheviks previously and was now legalized by the Soviet. Soldiers loyal to the Soviet and the Provisional Government were sent to mingle with Kornilov's troops and spread fear and discontent among them.

It was an impressive demonstration of unity in the face of danger. Railway workers refused to handle Kornilov's troop trains, telegraph operators would not dispatch his orders, workers in Petrograd threw up street barricades and settled down grimly to fight.

But the fight never came. Kornilov's troops deserted him, group by group, until only a handful were left and the Provisional Government succeeded in arresting him along with the others. The attack was averted, the danger past.

But there was a new danger to take its place. Since the Bolsheviks had thrown their support to the government during the crisis and had won greater popularity than ever, Kerensky was forced to include some of them in the new cabinet he formed. By the middle of September, they had also won control of the Petrograd Soviet; within days, the Moscow Soviet passed into their hands and, one by one, the others throughout the country were headed by members of the Bolshevist faction.

Lenin, still in Finland, kept in touch with Trotsky, newly elected chairman of the Petrograd Soviet, through messages carried by Stalin and others. One thread ran through all of them: the time is coming for the Bolsheviks to seize power—*all* the power—and members must learn now to accept party policy without criticism and obey all orders and decisions without question.

Then in October, Lenin himself returned to the capital, wearing a wig and facial make-up for disguise. Even while hiding, he issued a steady stream of pamphlets to try to win other party leaders to his view that the time had come for the Bolsheviks to drive "Kerensky and Company" from power. After ten hours of debate at a secret meeting held October 23, the vote was taken. Only Kamenev and Zinoviev were against him; Stalin, Trotsky and the others agreed that it was time for action.

A Political Bureau, or Politburo, was formed to act as general staff for the coming revolution. Trotsky, who had just been elected chairman of the Soviet's new Military Revolutionary Committee, which was to organize troops for the defense of the capital against the Germans, was to serve as a member of the Politburo, as were Lenin, Stalin, Zinoviev and Kamenev.

But regardless of the precautions the Bolsheviks took, word reached Kerensky of the plot.

"Let them try to overthrow the government," Kerensky told his informers. "I'd welcome the chance to crush them once and for all."

When his staff tried to tell him of the danger, he merely shrugged and repeated his statement. When a loyal citizen turned up at the palace with a letter in Lenin's own handwriting describing the planned coup, Kerensky refused to see him. His assistant looked over the letter without surprise.

"The situation is very grave, I know," he told the astounded citizen, "but Kerensky doesn't believe it. He doesn't want to believe it. His party leaders don't believe it. They're all perfectly sure that the Bolsheviks will never attempt to seize power."

"But Kerensky is not a stupid man?" the citizen asked.

The assistant sighed. "It's a sad story," he said. "He's a changed man. He shrinks from reality when it's unpleasant. No, there's no sense in your seeing Kerensky. He wouldn't pay any attention to your warning and you might irritate him."

So the Bolsheviks continued to plan. They had the troops now, in the form of the Red Guard. They had control of the Soviets. Their support from the masses seemed to be growing daily. The Provisional Government was shakier than ever, Kerensky less and less popular with the people.

Like a snake lying in wait behind a bush, they coiled, ready to strike when the precise moment came.

★ EIGHT

For two weeks the Military Revolutionary Committee of the Petrograd Soviet had worked diligently. In the third floor back room of the Smolny Institute, the old, palace-like building that had once been a school for the daughters of the nobility, Leon Trotsky and his staff had pored over maps, discussed strategy and laid plans. Now they were ready.

The first step was taken on November 4, 1917. The Military Revolutionary Committee issued a proclamation accusing the Provisional Government of serving counterrevolutionary interests, or working to take away the freedoms the people had won by overthrowing the Tsar. They also called on the soldiers of the Petrograd garrison to ignore all orders except those coming from the Soviet. Now there was nothing to do but sit back and wait.

They did not have long. Alexander Kerensky was furious.

"At every opportunity, the Bolsheviks have stood in the way of order and reason," he told a cabinet meeting the next day. "This is the last straw. We must take action against them."

The ministers of the cabinet agreed. Orders were issued to arrest the Bolshevik leaders and wreck their printing presses so there could be no more of the inflammatory newspapers and pamphlets.

It was cold that night, with a raw, damp wind blowing out of the west. On the surface, all was as usual. There were people in the streets, the streetcars ran, the theaters and cafes were open, the street lights burned brightly all over town. But there were other, more subtle, indications that something was wrong. It was in the wind; people seemed to sense it. They clustered in groups on street corners, talking nervously, starting at each sudden sound.

Meanwhile Kerensky prepared to end the Bolshevik threat "once and for all." Government troops were sent to wreck their printing presses and arrest them. The *Aurora,* a battleship in Petrograd harbor whose sailors were known to be Bolshevik sympathizers, was ordered out to sea. Telephone lines to the Smolny Institute were cut. A contingent of shock troops was ordered to come from Tsarskoye Selo, a short distance away. And the drawbridges across the Neva River which bisected Petrograd and separated the Government buildings from the workers' districts were ordered raised at four in the afternoon.

There were no guards posted at Smolny yet; it would have been an easy matter to take Leon Trotsky into custody. But the troops did not try. After halfheartedly damaging a few of the Bolshevik printing presses at various places around the city, they returned to their barracks.

But it was enough. The Bolsheviks had not wanted to be cast into the roles of villains, attempting to overthrow the government; they wanted to appear as the saviors of the people, the dedicated men who had fought against the injustice and persecution of a dictator. They had not wanted to make the first move. Now they did not have to. It was time to strike.

Lenin still lay in hiding in Vyborg, a few miles away across the Finland border. He had been informed of the plans but he had been warned, too, that it would be too dangerous for him to come to Petrograd just yet. In his room, he paced up and down like a caged tiger. What were they doing now? Had it all started? Were they going ahead without him?

Finally, he could stand it no longer. He had heard that the drawbridges were being raised, and to get to Smolny, he must cross one of those bridges. Danger or not, he had to go. He donned the wig Stalin had brought him, tied a handkerchief around his jaw as though he were suffering from a toothache, crowned the whole masquerade with a workman's cap and set out. With him was Eino Rahja, a young Finn. In case they were stopped by a patrol, Eino was to tell them his friend had a toothache and couldn't talk.

It was dark and cold. They hurried through the nearly empty streets, listening for patrols, avoiding the bright lights. There was one bridge Lenin felt might still be down and luck was with them. The last streetcar of the night was clanging shut its doors as they rushed up and boarded it.

On the other side of the river, they were on foot again, moving as stealthily as they could. Suddenly around the corner ahead of them, a patrol of cadets from the officers' training schools appeared.

"Go on," Eino whispered to Lenin. "I will deal with them."

Lenin disappeared like a shadow in the dark. Eino began singing loudly, pretending to be drunk. The cadets stopped him, looked at his papers, then let him go in disgust. They had better things to do that night than play caretaker to a drunken worker!

By the time Lenin reached Smolny, guards had been posted at both the outer gates and the door to the building. Machine guns were being set in place on either side of the huge double doors. There was a little difficulty over his disguise, but he was rescued by Trotsky and filled in on the events thus far.

They had taken the bridges first, while Lenin was on his way, knowing how vital they would be in allowing the Soviet members to move back and forth. All printing presses except those belonging to the Bolsheviks had been seized so that the Provisional Government would be unable to put out news of what was going on. Now squads were being sent to the telegraph agency, the post office, the telephone exchange and the State Bank. Everything was proceeding according to Trotsky's plan.

Earlier that day, Kerensky had frantically issued an order: "I command all military units and detachments to remain in their barracks until further orders. All officers who act without orders from their superiors will be court-martialed for mutiny. I forbid absolutely any execution by soldiers of instructions from their organizations."

What did Trotsky have to say? the reporters from the world-wide press services wanted to know. Trotsky let a smile flicker across his face. "The Petrograd Soviet feels that at last the moment has arrived when the power must fall into the hands of the Soviets," he answered.

Lenin smiled, too, as Trotsky brought him up to date on their progress. The lines of tension and fatigue that had creased his face before seemed to be gone. He was suddenly a whirlwind of activity. All his life had been directed toward this moment, this moment he had sometimes doubted would ever come.

By dawn, every key building was in Bolshevik hands except Maryinsky Palace, where the Council of the Republic, an advisory group to the government, was meeting, and the Winter Palace, where Kerensky and the Cabinet were still holding out. They had fallen without a fight. At the railroad station, the government guards had evaporated into the night at the sight of the Red Guards. Food warehouses had been seized, also. Bolsheviks had appeared at the jails and prisons with lists already drawn up of prisoners who were to be released. The *Aurora* was ordered to move back into the harbor, as close to the city as possible.

A short while later, Red Guards took Maryinsky Palace, breaking in on a debate by Council members about whether or not they should brand the new revolution as criminal. The guards ordered them to leave immediately or be arrested. The resolution was passed and the Council dispersed. Now there was only the Winter Palace left.

Inside the Palace, the Cabinet ministers were gathered around a long, green-draped table, discussing their predicament. It was not as hopeless as the Bolsheviks seemed to think. For one thing, the Bolsheviks had no knowledge of the private telephone line that still connected the Palace with a young officer in the attic of the Ministry of War. Besides the telephone line, the officer also had telegraph communications with the troops on the front line and was sending urgent messages for help. In addition, Kerensky had been able to commandeer a car from the American Embassy and, under the protection of the American flag, had escaped to the south, where he was trying to get help for the Provisional Government. So the ministers waited. For protection, they had several groups of cadets and the Women's Battalion, a military unit of women volunteers.

At two that afternoon, the atmosphere of bustle and confusion at Smolny was multiplied by the arrival of the members of the Soviet for an emergency meeting. The long, dim halls echoed with the stomping of feet and loud voices shouting greetings. Under the white chandeliers of the great meeting hall, clouds of stale cigarette smoke swirled in the stagnant air as the delegates packed themselves in, filling every seat, the window sills, even the aisles. Fur-hatted workers in black peasant blouses, soldiers in dull uniforms, some with rifles slung over their shoulders, talked, called out to each other, waited for their leaders.

At last, Kamenev appeared, making his way through the crowd, a bulging briefcase under his arm. Zinoviev, Lenin, then Trotsky followed.

Trotsky mounted the dais and, ignoring the fact that the Winter Palace and the ministers had still not surrendered, made again the announcement he had made at ten that morning: "The Provisional Government has fallen! The Revolution has been won!" The sea of faces in front of him broke into broad smiles and a wave of applause like thunder reverberated around the hall. He stood silently, accepting their tribute. It was his moment, his hour. The others spoke briefly, then left. There were many things to be done.

First, a cordon was set up around the Winter Palace. Armored cars, antiaircraft guns, field artillery and two thousand troops made an all but impregnable circle for any defense forces to pass through. The *Aurora* was brought up the Neva River so that the Palace was now in range of her guns. All was in readiness for the final attack.

The same scene was taking place in Moscow and dozens of other cities throughout Russia. The Soviets all over the country had attacked the existing government at the same moment, by the same timetable. But nowhere else had they been as successful as in Petrograd. In Moscow, government forces had put up a valiant fight and no one could guess yet which way it would go. There was scattered fighting in most of the provincial capitals; and in Georgia and Ukraine, the two southernmost provinces, the government forces seemed to have the upper hand.

As night came on, it grew colder and the marshy land on which Petrograd was built was mushy with ice. In the courtyard of Smolny Institute, the bonfires built by the Red Guards were reflected eerily on the sides of the armored cars pulled up under the trees, their motors idling, ready to move at the first command. A steady stream of traffic flowed through the gates—cars, trucks and whining motorcycles, in use now to carry messages until the telephone lines could be repaired.

At nine o'clock, the Winter Palace had still not surrendered. Trotsky sent word to the *Aurora* to fire on it. But use blanks, he added hastily. If they thought they were being attacked, they would become frightened and give up. The sailors on the *Aurora* began to ready the guns.

In contrast to Smolny, where every light seemed to be burning twice as brightly as before, the Winter Palace presented a dark, expressionless face to the Red Guards encircling it. There was no sign of life; nothing moved; the only sounds were made by the guards themselves. The *Aurora* finished cranking its guns into position, loaded them with blank shells and fired.

The answer was quick and short. From the Palace came the rapid bark of machine-gun fire. The guards, suddenly alert, brought their rifles up and fired blindly at the doors, windows, every place a gunner might be hidden within the dark Palace. The exchange lasted for an hour or so; then quiet descended again.

At one o'clock in the morning, the Red Guards decided on another maneuver. Singly, or in small groups, they began silently to infiltrate the Palace. One man, two or three, moved stealthily across the courtyard and disappeared into the dark maw of a doorway, then another and another. At last, some of the invaders encountered the cadet guards inside. Unable to tell friend from foe in the darkness, the two groups skirmished in the halls, but there were too many of the Red Guards and too few of the cadets. Forced to surrender, the cadets emerged from the building in groups of two and three.

"Now will you take up arms against the people?" a rough voice asked them as they reached the outside. Terrified by their grizzled conquerors, they managed a "no" and were sent on their way.

Inside, the search continued for the missing ministers and Kerensky. The Bolshevik leaders threw open door after door until they found the ministers in an inside room. "You are under arrest," one of the Bolsheviks said brusquely. They obediently stood up and began to file out.

The table they left behind bore mute evidence of their growing hopelessness as the night had progressed. At each place was a pad of paper, pen and ink. On the pads were rough drafts of manifestoes, proclamations, defense plans, counterattacks; then as the end had neared, there were simply meaningless scribbles.

News of the fall of the Winter Palace had spread quickly through the city, and by the time the ministers were led into the courtyard, a huge crowd had gathered to greet them. From somewhere in the crowd, an ugly voice called out, "Lynch them!" The ministers cowered more closely to their captors. Amid catcalls and jeers, demands for hanging, insults of every kind, the sailor guards pushed the ministers on through the crowd and into the waiting vehicles. They were to be taken to Peter and Paul Fortress, a rocky prison that stood on an island in Petrograd Harbor, where they would be safe from the crowds.

But there was still no trace of Kerensky. Red Guards searched the Palace thoroughly, looking not only for him but for anything else that might be of assistance. Every desk and cabinet was ransacked. The crowd outside began pushing in, too, gathering up the furnishings and other valuables, and preparing to carry them out. Two soldiers began ripping the red Spanish leather upholstering from the chairs, explaining to passers-by that they needed it for boots. Palace servants, carry-overs from the days of the Tsar, stood about in bewilderment, their spruce blue and red uniforms an odd contrast to the ragged mob. "You can't go in there. It is forbidden," they kept repeating.

The Red Guards, finished with their own search, now turned their attention to the crowds and began putting a stop to the looting. Stationing a part of their number at each doorway, they herded the others out, searching each person who left and taking away his plunder.

Within an hour, the lights had come on again on Nevsky Prospect, the city's main street. Here and there, squads of Red Guards and soldiers sat or squatted around small campfires. The cannons that had earlier threatened the street were now gone and, except for the soldiers, all was quiet and peaceful.

Not far away, in the City Duma building, another important event was taking place, unknown to the Bolsheviks, unnoted by the rest of the town. A small group of men, determined anti-Bolsheviks, were meeting. It took only minutes to pledge themselves to defeat the Bolsheviks and to agree on the name "The Committee of Salvation" and, with plans already made for a later meeting, to adjourn.

The city of Petrograd awoke as usual that morning of November 8, 1917. Thousands of workers climbed from their beds, ate their customary breakfasts, and went on their way to work as though nothing extraordinary had happened. Shops were open, factory furnaces puffed smoke at the winter sky, streetcars clanged their way through the streets. Nowhere did men gather in milling mobs as they had done six months ago when Nicholas had been overthrown. It was a day like any other day—except for an air of waiting, of expectancy, as though no one knew quite what had happened, as though they were all waiting to be told.

Only at Smolny was the air of revolution apparent. Dirt-

stained men, hollow-eyed from lack of sleep, rushed about
in the halls. Lenin, joined now by Krupskaya, who had come
from Vyborg, reappeared. He had napped briefly on a
blanket thrown carelessly on the floor. But he had been too
excited to sleep for long despite his almost overpowering
fatigue and, with daylight, had insisted on returning to work.
A desk and writing materials were found for him. He wrote
furiously throughout the long day, stopping only occasionally
to talk with someone or to rest a moment. There was so
much to be done. It was all there in his mind, the plans that
he had spent his life formulating. Now they had to be put
on paper.

Trotsky, too, worked at feverish pitch. All their military
gains must now be secured. The people must be informed
that the power now lay in the hands of the Soviet. The
isolated victories must be woven into complete control of
the government, not just in Petrograd, but throughout the
country.

At 8:40 P.M., another meeting of the Soviet began. In odd
moments snatched from the day's activities, Lenin, Trotsky
and a handful of loyal Bolsheviks had planned what must be
done. Now they must do it. Many of the other Bolsheviks
had argued that an all-Socialist government including members from the other Socialist parties must be formed. Lenin
and Trotsky held out. Only Bolsheviks must have a role
now, they insisted. The others were too unreliable; they
would not stand by the program the Bolsheviks had set up.

This was the message brought to the meeting by Trotsky,
standing before the tattered crowd in a black silk coat and
flowing tie. Only those who accepted the Bolshevik program
were welcome, he told them, his face pale with excitement
and fatigue. In the audience, many Mensheviks and Social Revolutionaries stood up and began making their way
through the noisy mob to the doors.

Kamenev was next. In a clear voice, he told the Soviet
delegates what had been done by the Military Revolutionary
Committee. Then came Lenin.

He mounted the dais and stood before them, a rather

small man, partly bald, rather unimpressive in appearance. But at that moment, he was not just the man—he was the legend, too. The man who had believed always in the revolution, the man who had preached it, the man who had lived for it. A wave of excitement caught the crowd and the applause broke like a sudden thunderstorm, rolling through the hall, echoing from the walls, repeated in the cheers and shouts of the worshiping multitude before him.

He stood quietly until it had ended. In his hoarse voice, he said to them, "We shall proceed now to construct the Socialist order." A small smile played across his mouth as the delegates again applauded. In the same harsh tone, he read his proposals for constructing that order.

He stated them so simply that it took a few moments for his audience to realize how radical they were. First he asked the Soviet to ratify a three-month armistice with Russia's enemies in the war so that just and democratic peace negotiations could be undertaken. There was a loud burst of applause when he finished; then an eerie kind of hush fell. The huge hall, filled to overflowing with turbulent humanity, was as quiet as a cemetery. A feeling of strangeness, of awe, seemed to sweep through the room; then, from somewhere, a lone voice was raised in the Funeral March, the song the revolutionaries had adopted as their own. The single voice became a torrent of sound as the others joined in.

"Farewell, brothers, you chose a noble path.
At your grave we swear to fight, to work for freedom and the people's happiness."

When the song was over and the silence had again descended, Lenin read his decree on land. Private property was to be abolished, without compensation to the owners. Church lands and estates were to be taken over and held by the local Soviets until a plan for them could be put into effect.

It was two in the morning when the debate finally ended and the land decree was put to a vote. The proposal for an armistice had passed unanimously; only one delegate voted against Lenin's recommendation for land. The peasant delegates danced wildly and hugged each other joyfully over its passage. At last, they thought, the land was to be theirs.

At two-thirty, Kamenev read the decree on the Constitution of Power, which would establish a committee to run the government until regular elections could be held. The Council of People's Commissars, it was to be called. It passed by an overwhelming majority. Lenin was then elected President, Trotsky, Commissar for Foreign Affairs, and Stalin, short, stocky, swarthy-faced Stalin, was to be Commissar of Nationalities.

It had been done; a beginning had been made. And now it was time to adjourn so that the delegates could take the news home to their various groups, news that the revolution was over, the Soviets were in power.

But news was already being circulated. And it was news of a totally different kind. Even while the Soviet had sat in session, passing its decrees, the Committee of Salvation, which had been joined now by many Mensheviks, Social Revolutionaries and some unions, had been hard at work flooding Petrograd and the rest of Russia with handbills which proclaimed a new Provisional Government and called on the citizens to disobey the orders of the Soviets. And there was a rumor that Kerensky had made his way to the front and was finding support among some of the troops there. It was not all over yet.

In response to the appeal from the Committee of Salvation, the government employees, including the postal workers, and the telegraph operators went on strike the next day. If the Bolsheviks wanted messages sent and delivered, they shrugged, let them do it themselves. The other citizens of Petrograd seemed to be waiting, to make sure they would be on the winning side.

In Moscow, the fighting had grown increasingly bitter. Soviet forces had taken the Kremlin, the huge complex of government buildings closed in by a high wall, then had lost it to a superior force of Cossacks and cadets. Cadets also held

Writers
of the
Communist
Manifesto

Engels

Marx

Trotsky

Stalin

Lenin

The Soviet
Leaders

Khrushchev

The Kremlin Moscow

the telephone and telegraph lines. Street fighting flared almost constantly.

And Kerensky was just twenty miles from Petrograd, at Gachina, with Cossacks under General Krasnov's command. Within the city, counterrevolutionaries had begun to attack Soviet patrols and there were skirmishes throughout the day between cadets and Red Guards.

Trotsky was a whirlwind of action. At his command, Red Guards began surrounding the various officers' schools, headquarters for the cadets. Soldiers, sailors, even factory workers were given arms and sent to guard the routes into Petrograd from the south. Others were issued spades and ordered to dig trenches. Trotsky himself visited the impromptu army in the field, cheering them on and bracing them for the attack by Kerensky's forces.

The attack never came. A few days later, on the heights of Pulkovo, a suburb of Petrograd, Kerensky, Krasnov and the contingents of Cossacks approached the line that had been dug by the Soviet forces. Behind the curtain of rain, the defenses looked formidable. The attackers hesitated, then stopped. Here and there, skirmishes between troops took place, but for the most part, the Cossacks, who had been infiltrated by agitators, had no heart to fight. Many of them simply disappeared. When the Red leaders offered the rest of them safe conducts which would permit them to return to their homes in southern Russia, most of them surrendered. When Trotsky arrived again at the front on the night of the thirteenth of November, the few remaining troops along with Kerensky and Krasnov were retreating.

They were captured in Gachina, a few miles farther south. While Kerensky sat in the next room, the Cossacks who had stayed with him bargained with the Bolsheviks for terms. For him it was a black moment. What was to happen to him now? As he sat stoically, awaiting his fate, the door opened and two young men, a soldier and a sailor, entered. They are here to arrest me, he thought quickly. Instead, they pulled out articles of clothing, a sailor's hat and coat, automobile goggles, which they made him put on. Together, the three of them slipped out the back, unnoticed by the bickering troops. There was an open space to cross to get to the gates. They made it, only to be confronted by a guard. One of the rescuers suddenly moaned and pretended to faint, a few feet from the guard, who rushed toward him. Kerensky slipped through the gates, into a waiting automobile, onto the first lap of the journey that would carry him safely to Paris.

In Moscow, the fighting had become increasingly desperate. Lights and telephones were out. Machine-gun fire swept the main streets almost continuously. Cadets and White Guards (the name given those who opposed the Bolsheviks, or Red Guards) were still holding the Kremlin, the strategic center of the city.

The Military Revolutionary Committee of the Moscow Soviet rolled its heaviest guns into position, then delivered its ultimatum: "Surrender or be bombarded."

The cadets and the White Guards surrendered. Now Moscow belonged to the Bolsheviks and the Soviet.

At Tsarskoye Selo, as at many other towns, the Soviet moved in and took possession. They went from house to house, searching for enemies, consolidating their control. Once they found an old man, ill in bed. He was unknown to them and they searched his house hurriedly and went on to the next one. George Plekhanov, the founder of the Russian Social Democratic Party, which had given birth to the Bolsheviks, was too old and too ill to argue with them.

In Petrograd and in Moscow, the Russian Orthodox priests exhorted the people to resist, to fight off this new invader who was more of a threat to them than the Tsar had ever been. Word reached the Red Guards and one of the priests was seized and shot, as an example. The Bolsheviks were determined to cut off any counterrevolutionary movement at its beginning. First the Tsar, then the Provisional Government had made many mistakes in dealing with them; they would not make those same mistakes in dealing with their enemies.

No one in Russia believed that the Bolsheviks could hold

power longer than a few days. No one, that is, except Lenin and Trotsky, and perhaps a few of the more simple-minded among the Red Guards.

Only time would tell which of them was right.

NINE

I**T WAS THE COLDEST WINTER ON RECORD. D**AY **AFTER DAY,** the temperature stayed below zero; the gray sky was heavy with low clouds; a biting, bitter wind drove the cold into one's bones. On January 18, 1918, the day the Constituent Assembly was to meet for the first time, the snow began again, thick, dense, covering everything in deep blankets.

In Petrograd that morning, the people were troubled and apprehensive, as though they were expecting something new and even more dreadful to happen.

"What will the Bolsheviks do now?" they whispered to one another.

"What can they do?" a tall, bearded man asked. "After all, we showed them in the election last month where they stand. The people do not want them."

"Some of the people do," a fur-hatted worker retorted angrily.

"Barely a third," sneered the tall man. "They thought we would give them all the votes, and instead they got scarcely a third."

"But they still have control of the government, don't they?" a small woman with a frightened face said weakly. "How do we know they will let the others meet?"

"We will force them to, that's how!" a man near her replied. He lifted a sign he had been carrying at his side. "Down with the Bolsheviks!" it read.

"That's the spirit!" someone called. Other signs appeared from beneath people's coats. "Away with tyrants!" "Down with the Reds!"

As though a signal had been given, the crowds started moving toward Nevsky Prospect, the main street of Petrograd. It was eleven o'clock in the morning.

"To the palace!" someone called out. Others took up the cry. "To the palace!" The crowd started moving slowly down the wide street in the direction of the palace where the Assembly was to meet.

It was difficult to walk against the icy wind, even more difficult to see in the blizzardlike snow that fell constantly. The front rows of marchers were just a few blocks from their goal when they saw some sort of obstruction in the street in front of them. Other marchers they supposed, and kept moving, straining to see ahead of them.

Through the swirling snow they could finally see—soldiers—five hundred of them, lined up across the street. In front of them stood twenty machine guns. A few of the marchers hesitated, almost stopped.

"They will not fire," a voice called from the crowd. "We are unarmed."

The soldiers were silent and the people kept walking. There were thirty thousand of them, all unarmed. They moved steadily closer. Now there was just fifty feet between them.

On command, the machine guns came suddenly to life. There were screams and shouts, shrieks from the wounded. Two factory workers fell, still clutching a sign which read "Down with the murderers of democracy!" Those in front surged back but the pressure from the rear forced them forward. Again and again, the machine guns barked. More fell, dead or wounded. The people turned and fled, away from the palace, away from this horrible slaughter. Whatever they had thought before, they knew now that the Bolsheviks were determined to hold the power they had seized by whatever means they felt necessary.

The city was still buzzing like an angry beehive when the Assembly finally convened that afternoon. The delegates came quietly and courageously, not knowing what their fate would be. Most of them carried sandwiches and candles, expecting that the Bolsheviks might turn out the lights to force them into adjourning.

By early afternoon they had assembled—all except the Bolsheviks. Where were they? the other delegates wondered. Shortly after two, Lenin and Krupskaya were seen driving up to a side door. The delegates breathed a sigh of relief. *This* was what the Bolsheviks had been waiting for—the arrival of their leader. *Now* they would come. The others had been reluctant to begin without them, afraid of the action the Bolsheviks might take when they did arrive.

But still they did not come. Through the closed door to a side room they could hear occasional laughter, the rattle of teacups, low conversation. They waited anxiously. The balconies were filling with spectators, mostly soldiers and sailors who were in an obvious state of excitement, expecting something to happen.

At four o'clock, the side door opened and Lenin came in, followed by the other Bolsheviks. As the others took their seats, Lenin walked toward the speaker's platform and settled himself on the red-carpeted stairs. The meeting could now begin.

The first order of business was the election of a chairman. The Bolsheviks nominated a candidate; someone rose and proposed the name of one of the right-wing Social Revolutionaries. On the steps, Lenin seemed completely indifferent but the spectators raised an immediate outcry. A vote was taken. Amid shouts and insults from the balconies, the delegates elected the Social Revolutionary.

As the new Chairman took his place at the platform, the delegates watched Lenin. It would appear that he had taken that position so that he could signal—but to whom, and why? Would there be an attack by the armed soldiers and sailors on the balconies? Would it be the guards? And *when?*

As if in answer, Lenin rose and sauntered casually over to one of the front seats and sat down. A Bolshevik delegate walked to the platform and presented a motion with the Bolsheviks' program for the new government. The spectators cheered loudly and raucously. Courageously, one of the Social Revolutionaries presented a program in opposition.

"The Bolsheviks are interlopers and wreckers," he said. "They are trying to take the power that belongs rightly to the people."

A soldier leaped from the low balcony, pulling his gun as he landed, and raced to the platform.

"Do you see this?" he asked, waving the revolver in the speaker's face. The delegates in the audience gasped.

From the corner of his eye, the speaker saw the weapon. His face went white but his voice did not waver. The soldier stood there uncertain for a moment, then laughed and returned to the balcony. The audience seemed to sigh with relief. The crisis was averted for the moment.

But only for the moment. When a vote was taken, the delegates chose the program proposed by the Social Revolutionaries. What would the Bolsheviks do now?

It was almost one o'clock in the morning. They had been in session constantly for nine hours. Someone called for a recess and they all agreed. One of the Bolsheviks jumped to his feet.

"It is not a recess—it is an adjournment," he shouted. "The Assembly is a farce and does not represent the people. The Bolsheviks are leaving!"

With Lenin leading the way, the Bolsheviks walked out of the room. The other delegates took a short recess, then reconvened. It was becoming increasingly difficult to hear the speakers because of the noise from the spectators' galleries. The soldiers and sailors were amusing themselves by shouting, stomping their feet, and pointing rifles at each speaker. Despite the danger and the distractions, the delegates went doggedly on, duty bound to do what they could to bring some kind of legitimate government to Russia.

The sergeant of the guards looked at his watch. Four-thirty in the morning. He glanced around at the other guards. They were leaning against the walls, yawning, their rifles held loosely at their sides. He had had enough of this, he decided. Didn't these fools know that nothing they did mattered anyway?

"Adjourn the meeting," he called out to the Assembly Chairman.

"We are about to vote on the land reform bill," the Chairman answered. "We cannot adjourn until then."

"You'll adjourn or we'll adjourn you by turning out the lights," the sergeant threatened.

The delegates ignored him, but the other guards came to life. "That's enough," the one at the door yelled. "Get out of here!" Others took up the chorus. "Get out! Get out!"

The Chairman asked for a vote on the measure. As he counted the hands, the lights went out, leaving the Assembly in total darkness.

Afraid to light their candles and become clear targets for the armed soldiers, the delegates stumbled and felt their way outside to the foggy street. Once there, in the frozen light of a wan moon and an occasional street light, they dispersed quickly and quietly, each of them sure that the Bolsheviks would search him out and wreak revenge on all of them for the independence of their actions. But regardless of the consequences, they felt a thrill of pride. They had participated in free debate in a freely elected assembly. It was the only instance in Russian history and it would probably not happen again.

Lenin and Trotsky reviewed the event the next morning. "It was a mistake to let them meet," Lenin said. "I thought that they would give us their support, knowing that we hold the power."

Trotsky shook his head. "They are stubborn men," he replied.

The rest of the population was almost equally stubborn. Ignoring the Bolshevik decree to nationalize land, the peasants were simply helping themselves. The workers, too, were in an uproar.

"Why should the owners fatten themselves on our labor?" a shop foreman asked his fellow workers. "Are we not the ones who make the furniture? All they do is sit in an office and reap the profits while we do the work."

"That's right," a chorus of growls answered him.

"I say 'Throw them out!' " he yelled.

"We're with you! Throw them out!" the workers roared. They advanced on an office where a hapless owner sat going over his books. "We'll run the factory ourselves!"

Production dwindled to nearly a standstill as the scene was repeated all over Russia. It picked up again when the workers discovered they could not run the factories without managers, and so they hired the former owners back to run the factories.

In addition to their problems at home, the Bolsheviks faced yet another one, a most crucial one. They had promised a quick and final end to the war as a part of their program. Germany had agreed to a truce to discuss a permanent peace but the terms she offered were outrageous: all Russian land invaded by Germany was to be kept by her to do with as she pleased. That would include Poland, Estonia, Latvia and Lithuania. Georgia and the Ukraine, the two southern provinces, were to be independent. Some areas in the south were to go to Turkey. One and a quarter million square miles, sixty-two million people, one third of Russia's farm land, one half of her industrial plants and equipment, four fifths of her iron, and ninety per cent of her coal were to be taken from her.

"This is not peace, it is ruin," Leon Trotsky told the German representative. "We cannot possibly accept such a bargain."

The German smiled. "Do you have a choice?" he asked blandly.

On February 18, the answer came. Germany resumed the war. Lenin appointed Trotsky to raise an army to replace the one that had evaporated during the truce and sent other representatives to talk again with the Germans.

"Make what terms you can," he instructed them, "but stop the war. We have no army and no defense. It is better to lose part of the nation than all of it."

The Germans refused to soften the terms and the Treaty of Brest-Litovsk, signed March 3, 1918, was based on their first offer. The Bolsheviks would need no army now to fight the Germans, but there were rumors that they would need it to fight anti-Bolshevik forces which were gathering in the outlying provinces. And they might need it for protection against their former Allies. Disturbed about Russia's withdrawal from the war and disapproving of the Bolshevik program, the Allies were landing troops at various ports in Russia and were reported to be joining with the White, or anti-Bolshevik, forces.

More immediately, the loss of the Ukraine, the bread-basket of Russia, was sure to mean a serious food shortage. The loss of half of the industrial plants, coupled with the frivolous attitude of the workers, meant that production had virtually collapsed.

Despite the gravity of the situation, Lenin pushed ahead with the Bolshevik program. A law providing for the drafting of workers was passed. Inheritance of private property was abolished. The Gregorian calendar, the one used by the Western World, including America, was adopted to replace the old Russian calendar, which had been two weeks behind the Gregorian. The capital was moved from Petrograd to Moscow and the government officials were housed in the Kremlin, the ancient walled city within a city. And the Bolsheviks officially adopted the name *Communist Party*, a name Lenin felt reflected their ideas better than the old Socialist Democratic title.

The next crisis came in May. The Austrian government, Russia's enemy in the war, had drafted Czechoslovakians into the army but they had proved to be unsatisfactory soldiers. Rather than fight for the Austrian emperor whom they detested, they had surrendered en masse to the Russians. A group of about forty-five thousand had been held in Russia as prisoners of war. During the truce between Russia and Germany and Austria, the Czechs had been accepted by the French army and arrangements had been made between the French and Bolshevik governments to send the

Czechs to Vladivostok, on Russia's Pacific coast, where the French would evacuate them.

But the Communists found that they could not spare that many trains to go that far away from the main centers of Russia and consequently, in late April, new orders were issued to turn those trains which had not gone too far around and route them instead to Archangel and Murmansk, on the northern Atlantic side of Russia.

No one thought to tell the Czech troops about the change in orders and, seeing the trains turned around and headed back in the same direction from which they had come, they became suspicious. At a stop in Chelyabinsk, in central Russia, the uneasy Czechs became involved in a brawl with a group of Hungarian p.o.w.'s. Moscow, informed by telegraph, ordered that the Czechs be disarmed immediately to stop the rioting.

Already suspicious that something contrary to their interests was going on, the Czechs refused to give up their weapons. Once again, Leon Trotsky was contacted by telegraph. His orders were brief and to the point. The Czech regiments were to be broken up and they were to be incorporated into the Red Guards or into collective labor groups.

"Every Czechoslovakian found armed on the railway line is to be shot on the spot," he ordered. "Every detachment in which there is even one armed man is to be detrained and locked up in a war prisoners' camp."

Informed of the order, the Czechs revolted in earnest. They seized a section of the railroad and set up armed camps all along it.

It was the opportunity the anti-Bolsheviks had been waiting for. Here were thousands of armed men, the nucleus of an army, in revolt against the Communists. Everywhere, under the protection of the Czechs, White (or anti-Communist) armies began to take shape. Two months later, they were receiving money, supplies and men from Russia's former allies, Great Britain, France and the United States.

As the armies began converging on Moscow, the Reds became increasingly desperate. Conscription was instituted to swell the Red Army. The Cheka redoubled its activities to try to halt subversion within the area the Communists held. Martial law was proclaimed in many districts. The period known as the Red Terror had come, a period in which hundreds of thousands lost their lives for no reason other than that they appeared not to agree with the Communists and their methods.

Nor were the areas under White control spared. The Whites had gathered under their banners all anti-Communists, regardless of who or what they were. Some were monarchists, ex-military men, Cossacks, Socialists who hated Communists, democrats, opportunists and adventurers. The army they collected was one of the cruelest and most savage on record, sometimes taking a village and torturing and killing its inhabitants for sport.

All of Russia was being dipped into a gigantic blood bath that would leave stains on its history forever.

In charge of the Red Army, Leon Trotsky traveled in a special train, moving constantly back and forth across Russia, visiting the troops, laughing with them, encouraging them, pushing them onward. He was a human dynamo, somehow able to breathe his own restless energy into others. Joseph Stalin was his opposite, slow, plodding, impassive in expression. Yet each had his value to Lenin and he found uses for the abilities of both. Trotsky headed the army; Stalin carried out less demanding but still important offices. In June, he was sent to Tsaritsyn, in southern Russia, to try to secure more food to relieve the tremendous shortage.

It was not the simple matter it had been thought to be. The Whites were particularly strong in the south and though Stalin was able to reach Tsaritsyn with no difficulty, he was unable to leave it. The Whites had taken all the surrounding area and were blocking his return to Moscow.

Stalin promptly set himself up as dictator of Tsaritsyn and showed little interest in trying to escape the White net. Trotsky was furious.

"Stalin is not trying to get back," he stormed at Lenin. "He is enjoying himself while we are waiting for him—

worse, while we are in desperate need of the grain he is supposed to bring back and the men he has tied up there."

"Do you really believe he could get back if he wanted to?" Lenin asked.

"I know he could," Trotsky answered hotly.

"Then we will order him back and find out," Lenin said.

Stalin made his way back to Moscow, stolid and silent as ever. Lenin talked to the two of them, smoothing over their hostility toward each other, convincing them that they must get along for the sake of the party. On the outside, all went on as usual. Trotsky seemed to shrug the whole matter off and forget it. But not Stalin; in his own eyes, he had been humiliated by Trotsky. It was an episode he would never forgive; the first spark of hatred had been struck and would not be put out again as long as Trotsky lived.

Lenin had bigger and more immediate worries. Despite their disunity, the White armies were advancing toward Moscow. If they should ever find common cause, how much more dangerous would they be? He shuddered as he remembered the royal family, the Romanovs, in exile at Ekaterinburg, straight in the path of the White advance. It would never do to let them fall into the hands of the Whites, where they would serve as a living symbol of the old Russia, a rallying point for all those who were dissatisfied with the Communists.

On the night of July 16, 1918, Nicholas Romanov, his wife, Alix, their children, their personal servants and the family physician were awakened and told to get dressed hurriedly. There were disturbances, the guards told them, it was necessary to remove the family to a place of safety immediately.

They tumbled out of bed and pulled their clothes on hastily. The servants rustled about and managed to make tea for the family. As they drank, they could hear soldiers entering the downstairs floor of the house. A few moments later, guards appeared again and led the family downstairs to a room where a row of chairs had been placed against one wall. One guard gestured toward the chairs and the family sat down, expectantly. Nicholas held his thirteen-year-old son on one knee; the others sat in separate chairs. Eleven soldiers lounged against the opposite wall.

There was hardly time to speculate on what was coming next when a messenger entered and handed Nicholas a paper. It was a death warrant for the family, signed by the local Soviet. Nicholas barely had time to glance at it when the head of the local political police stepped forward and took it from him.

"Your relatives abroad have been trying to save you but they have failed," he said haughtily. "I have orders from the Ekaterinburg Soviet to shoot you and your family."

Startled and horrified, Nicholas stood up quickly, supporting his son with one hand. Before he could cry out, the man lifted a revolver, pointed it at Nicholas' forehead and fired. Nicholas fell heavily to the floor. As the others began screaming, the soldiers opposite them raised their guns and began firing.

It was a scene from a fiendish nightmare. One by one, the Romanovs and their entourage fell. Bullets whined through the small room, ricocheting off its walls. One of the daughters fainted and came to only to find herself the last survivor. As she shrieked, the soldiers took aim again and she fell. The little dog she had been carrying began yelping in terror around her body. Again the soldiers raised their guns and the dog joined the heap of bodies on the bloody floor. At last, the screaming stopped, the guns were silent, the room was as quiet as the tomb it had become.

The Romanovs were no more; any threat they might have been to the Communists was gone forever. Trotsky summed it up later: "The execution of the Tsar's family was needed not only to frighten, horrify and dishearten the enemy but also to shake up our own ranks, to show them that there was no turning back, that ahead lay either complete victory or complete ruin."

And which it would be was by no means certain in the summer of 1918. The Whites continued advancing steadily. The Red Armies were falling back before them; famine was raging through the land. Then in August, another blow fell.

Lenin was attending a meeting at an industrial plant in a Moscow suburb. As was his custom, he had been driven there by Til, a combination chauffeur and secret police agent. After Lenin disappeared inside, Til lounged idly against the car, waiting his return and keeping an eye on the passers-by. He watched a young woman approach, making a mental note of her appearance. Late twenties, black hair, rather homely. Dark coat, no hat. She came within a few feet of him and stopped.

"Has Lenin arrived yet?" she asked courteously. She seemed quite calm, he noticed. Calm and reserved, that's how he would describe her.

"I don't know," he answered, as he usually did to all questions about Lenin from unknowns.

A smile brightened the girl's rather commonplace features. "I'm sure he's here," she said. She turned and walked toward the building.

She stopped briefly to exchange a few words with a tall, blond, clean-shaven young man, then disappeared inside the building and Til dismissed her from his mind. An hour later, he remembered the incident when he saw Lenin emerge from the building, the girl beside him in the crowd. She and Lenin were talking spiritedly as they approached the car. Til opened the car door, the group stopped and Lenin started to enter the car.

Suddenly five shots rang out, in rapid succession. Lenin stumbled and crumpled. Til caught him, holding him up. There were screams and shouts in the crowd. No one seemed to know who had been shot or who had done the shooting. In the confusion, the girl pushed her way through the crowd and began running down the street. Only then did the crowd become aware of what had happened. Some of the people ran after her, catching her as she neared a car parked on a side street. As the crowd overtook her, the tall, blond man inside gunned the motor and escaped.

Back by Lenin's car, someone called out frantically, "Get an ambulance!"

"No," Lenin said weakly to Til. "Take me home."

Til managed to get him back to the Kremlin. Four bullets had hit him, one through his lung, one in his neck, one hit his collarbone and broke it, one merely scratched his shoulder. For ten days he teetered between life and death, then gradually he began to recover. One bullet remained with him the rest of his life as a reminder of that August day and Fanny Kaplan.

She was not so fortunate. Turned over to the Cheka, the secret police arm of the government, by the crowd which had captured her, she admitted to the shooting. Her identity was quickly established. She was a Social Revolutionary and had spent eleven years in prison for attempting to assassinate a tsarist official. She had been freed in the general amnesty proclaimed by the Provisional Government after the March Revolution. That was all she told, despite ten months of questioning by the Cheka. Her accomplice was never caught. Convinced that they would never get any more out of her, the Cheka agents shot her.

But one life was not enough. Hundreds were lined up and executed without trial and without mercy by the Cheka. It was an attempt to terrorize the population and it was remarkably successful.

And as Lenin lay recuperating inside Kremlin walls, the White armies pushed closer and closer. By winter, life in Moscow had slowed almost to a standstill. Hunger and cold were twin phantoms that haunted the whole city, as well as the surrounding countryside. People fought in the streets like dogs over scraps of food. The power system was constantly failing, leaving the city without lights and with little heat. By the beginning of 1919, typhus, a deadly disease characterized by high fever, began taking its toll. Terror and typhus, hunger and cold fought for their victims. Exhausted from years of suffering and privation, people fell in the streets. In Moscow, the dead were stacked like logs in the cemeteries, waiting for the spring thaw when the ground would soften enough to bury them.

Then the tide turned for the Reds. World War I having

officially ended, the Allies could find no further excuse for keeping troops on Russian soil or for supplying the White armies. Even had they wanted to, they were facing mutiny from their own troops, who had had enough and were clamoring to go home. First the French, then the British and Americans began evacuating troops and stopping the flow of supplies. Slowly, tortuously, the Red armies pushed the Whites back. In 1920, the province of the Ukraine was recaptured and rejoined with Russia; early in 1921, Georgia, the last stronghold of the Whites, was retaken.

The Communists were in control. Private property had been abolished; all production nationalized. The banks had been closed to discourage any private trading at all. No one could estimate the total number of dead at the hands of the Communists and the Whites. No one could estimate how long it would be before Russia, as a nation, could function in anything like a normal fashion.

But whatever the cost, the Communists had done what they had set out to do. They were now in control.

★ TEN

By the end of winter, early in 1921, reports were coming in that enraged Lenin.

"Why is the food shortage becoming worse?" he shouted. "Are you not confiscating the surplus from the peasants as you were instructed?"

The official spread his hands in a gesture of futility. "They have quit producing a surplus since they know we will take it," he said. "If the harvest is better than expected, they destroy the extra food."

It was the same in other areas of national life. Production had fallen since private ownership had been outlawed. Religion had not disappeared with the persecution of its leaders. The withdrawal of money had not stabilized the economy. Nothing had worked according to plan.

"But the schools," Lenin persisted. "Surely the schools are better now that we have done away with discipline and the arbitrary authority of teachers?"

The commissar for education looked at the floor, avoiding Lenin's accusing eyes. "The students do not attend," he said. "The tests show that those who do are not learning."

Lenin slumped in his chair, a frown creasing his forehead. "I don't understand," he said after a moment. "The strikes, the looting—don't the people realize what we have done for them?"

The other officials kept silent. "Yes," he went on, "that's it. We have gone too far too fast. The people don't understand."

He repeated the statement to the Moscow Soviet on February 28, 1921. "We have gone too far too fast," he said

116

from the platform, "and it has been a mistake. We must make changes, give the people more time to understand communism and adjust to it."

The new program, or the New Economic Policy as it was called, was to be in effect a compromise between communism and capitalism. Instead of taking the peasants' surplus, the government would collect a tax on it. Smaller factories and businesses were to be returned to their former owners; the wage system was to be restored.

No compromise was to be made politically, however. The Cheka, the police organization formed out of the old Military Revolutionary Committee, was given strict orders to root out any elements of political opposition and do away with them. No criticism of any kind was to be allowed. In return for a small measure of economic freedom, the Russian people were to give up all political freedom whatsoever.

At first, the peasants were suspicious of the new rules, expecting to find a catch in them somewhere. Spring planting was done, but only enough sown to feed each family, so that at best it would be a while before there would be any food to trade or to tax. In the following months, as the peasants came to believe that the government meant what it said, Nature took a hand in defeating the Communists.

It was the worst year they could remember. Day after day, week after week, no rain fell and the ground lay parched and cracked. Dust storms swirled through the agricultural belt; then came the locusts. Anything that had escaped the elements fell victim now to the locusts that swarmed out of nowhere, stripped the fields bare and disappeared.

By fall, there was almost nothing to eat in all of Russia. By the thousands, people were dying of starvation. There was little question now of a revolt; few had the strength to lift a weapon. The peasants swarmed into the cities, searching for food, as the locusts had swarmed into the countryside.

In the Kremlin, Lenin, Krupskaya and his sister Maria limited themselves to a fraction of their normal diet. But it was only a gesture and he knew it. If everyone in Russia did the same, there still would not be enough food to go around.

"We must have help," he said. "But where can we get it?"

It came from the source he had least expected—from the United States and other capitalist countries. He had expected them to drown in the revolutionary tide he thought he had created. Instead, they were offering to feed his people.

Reluctantly, he accepted their help. "But feed only the children," he commanded. He did not need to tell them why. They were aware that he was afraid to have the adults come into contact with the Americans and other capitalist people who would be handling the distribution of the food, afraid that they would be "contaminated" by the ideas they might hear.

As the Communists struggled to consolidate their control over the country and the people fought off starvation, the lines in his face deepened into a permanent frown. The stress of the situation was beginning to tell on him.

"I—I am not well," he said one day.

Krupskaya looked up in time to see him grasp the back of a chair, reeling a little as he did so. She rushed to his side.

"What is it?" she asked anxiously. "Are you all right?"

It was a moment before he could answer. "A little dizzy, that's all," he said.

Krupskaya helped him to the bed. "I will call the doctor," she said firmly.

"No, no," he answered weakly. "I am all right. No need for doctors."

"We will have them anyway," she answered.

"No. I forbid it."

But the spells continued, and he agreed. The most competent doctors of Russia and Germany were called in for consultation. There was nothing organically wrong with him, they reported.

"Whatever the doctors say, I am ill," he told Krupskaya. "The spells are not in my mind. They are in my body."

"A change, that's what he needs," Krupskaya told Maria

privately. "There is too much noise and confusion here; he has worked too hard."

The three of them moved to Gorki, an estate twenty miles away on a hill surrounded by fields and woods.

"It is lovely and peaceful here," he told Krupskaya. "Surely it will bring peace to me, too."

But it did not. The headaches and the dizzy spells continued. Sometimes the pain was so excruciating that he was like a madman.

By March, 1922, when he attended the Eleventh Congress of the Communist Party in Moscow, he was a very sick man. His face was drawn and pale as he addressed the delegates.

"We must return to real communism," he told them. "We must find our way back to the doctrines of Karl Marx."

A new crop was in and the worst of the famine was past; the psychological effect of restoring some private ownership under the New Economic Policy had helped production considerably; but this was not the kind of state he had dreamed of and worked for.

He sponsored one other change at the Congress, this one successfully. He arranged for the election of Joseph Stalin as General Secretary of the Party. He neither liked nor trusted Stalin but he recognized the man's talents as an organizer. The Party could use him.

It could use Leon Trotsky, too. "I will arrange for your appointment as deputy chairman of the Council of Peoples' Commissars," he told Trotsky. "Should anything happen to me, you would be next in line and the government would be in good hands."

Trotsky thought about it for a moment. "No," he decided. "Not now." To himself he thought it might look as though he were trying to replace Lenin.

"Later, then," Lenin replied. "There is still time."

But time was running out. On May 26, Maria called the doctor in Moscow. She was frantic, and when he asked what had happened she said she thought it might be food poisoning. "We had fish last night and it did not taste too fresh."

"Did anyone else eat the fish?" the doctor asked.

"All of us."

"Is anyone else ill?"

"No, only Lenin."

"I will come at once." He took time only to gather up some colleagues, fearful that if anything happened to Lenin and he was the only doctor, he would be held responsible.

The doctors examined him carefully. He was vomiting, his head ached unbearably, his stomach was knotted with cramps.

They asked him questions but his answers were slurred and scarcely understandable. In a few moments, the doctors retreated to an outer room where they could talk.

"What is it? It is not serious, is it?" Krupskaya implored.

The doctors nodded. "Yes, I'm afraid it is," one of them told her. "We believe he has had a stroke and there is some brain damage. He must be put to bed immediately for total, complete rest. No visitors and no activities."

"For how long?" Krupskaya wanted to know.

The doctors looked at each other and shrugged. "Who can say?"

They had reckoned without the tremendous vitality of their patient. He had moved too long in a constant round of feverish activity.

"I am well now. I must get up. There is too much to be done for me to lie here in bed as though I were ill," he protested three weeks later.

"You are a very sick man," the doctor replied as he held a firm hand on Lenin's pulse. "There will be no getting up."

It was midsummer before the first visitors other than the family were allowed. Stalin and Kamenev came to see him.

"We bring good news," Stalin told him. "There will be a bumper harvest this year."

"The first since the revolution," Kamenev added.

Lenin smiled and was silent for a moment. "The hardest days are now behind us," he said.

They went on to talk of one thing and another on the

political scene—everything except Stalin's own activities. As General Secretary of the Party, he had contact with every local Party secretary and, during Lenin's illness, he had been slowly replacing them with men loyal only to himself. He, too, had his dreams of the future, and his were dreams of personal power and glory. When Lenin was gone, Joseph Stalin would be ready to step into his shoes.

Day by day, week after week, Lenin fought valiantly against his illness. By fall, he looked as though he had won. He had gained weight, his face had filled out, he was in good spirits. He made his first public appearance at a Party executive committee meeting.

The meeting was in progress when he entered at the back of the Great Kremlin Palace. Dressed in black trousers and a gray jacket, a bright blue necktie decorating his flannel shirt, he made his way slowly down the side of the hall. He was almost to the platform before he was recognized.

"It's Lenin," someone whispered. The word went from delegate to delegate until the whole room seemed to be filled with the sound of his name. The delegates rose to their feet, cheering.

He spoke to them briefly. "How well he looks!" they told each other. "Better than ever," they decided. They gave him another standing ovation when he finished. "It is the old Lenin back again," they said.

But three weeks later, when he spoke to the Moscow Soviet, his appearance had changed radically. The bloom of health and well-being had given way to a haggard, tired look. The doctors ordered him back to bed in the Kremlin.

"I am worse," he told Krupskaya the night of December 13. "I can feel myself slipping." Later that night, the vomiting and the nausea began again and, a little later, his headaches and insomnia became worse.

The doctors were frankly worried. "He must have absolute rest," they told Krupskaya. "No phone calls, no visitors, no reading—nothing but total and complete rest."

It seemed impossible in the Kremlin. Somehow, Krupskaya and Maria managed to get him back to Gorki. Then, three days later, he took a sudden and dramatic turn for the worse.

Krupskaya had to bend close to catch the words. "My arm," he said. "I can't move my right arm."

She called the doctors in panic.

"It is what we feared most," they told her after the examination. "It is another stroke."

"There are things I must do," Lenin told them. "I have some things to be put in order," he hesitated a moment, "in case my illness should catch me unaware."

The doctors talked it over. He was so agitated over not being able to work, perhaps his agitation would hurt him more than the work would.

"What is it you must do?" they asked him.

"Nothing exciting," he told them with the shadow of a grin, "just a kind of diary."

They agreed that he might dictate to a secretary for a brief period each day and he lay back with a sigh of relief. There were things that must be done, that *he* must do, before he could die, he knew now since his visit to the Kremlin. But the pain was agonizing; it took all his strength simply to get the words out.

"Comrade Stalin, having become General Secretary, has concentrated immeasurable power in his hands, and I am not sure that he always knows how to use that power with sufficient caution. On the other hand, Comrade Trotsky . . . is distinguished not only by his exceptional abilities . . . but also . . . by his excessive enthusiasm for the purely administrative aspect of his work."

It was obvious that during his stay in the Kremlin, he had discovered something about Stalin that made it necessary for him to risk his life now to see that Trotsky, not Stalin, inherited the leadership if he himself should die.

Part of it was the situation in the province of Georgia. Stalin, a native of Georgia, had been put in charge of bringing it into a closer relationship with the rest of the Soviet Union. His methods had been coercion, murder and worse.

It had been violence not for the sake of ends to be gained, but for its own sake. Lenin had been outraged when he learned of it.

It took three days and an untold measure of his strength to complete the dictation for the document that was to become known as his Last Testament. When it was finished, he lay back on his pillows, a grim half-smile on his face.

"You must tell no one, do you understand?" he told the secretary.

She nodded.

"Make five copies. One I will keep, three you will give to Krupskaya, one is to go in the secret file in my office," he ordered. "They will be ready when they are needed."

A few days later, he added a postscript.

"Stalin is too coarse, and this fault, though tolerable among us Communists, becomes unbearable in a General Secretary. Therefore, I propose to the comrades to find some way of removing Stalin from his position and appointing someone else who differs in all respects from Comrade Stalin . . . namely, someone more tolerant, more loyal, more polite and considerate to his comrades . . ."

It was as though he had finally realized that, of all his errors, the worst had been to allow Stalin a position of authority. Now he must try to rectify that error by assuring his removal.

The Georgian business seemed to prey on his mind, too. "Hundreds killed," he muttered, as though to himself, "thousands imprisoned needlessly." He rolled his head slowly from side to side. "I am, I believe, strongly guilty before the workers of Russia for not having intervened energetically or drastically enough," he wrote. It was a new Lenin, a more gentle Lenin, that was arising from his illness, one concerned with people as human beings rather than as a social experiment.

As his illness progressed, he brooded more and more over the possibility of the wily Stalin succeeding him when he died. Finally he could bear it no longer. He called Krupskaya to him and dictated a note to be delivered to Stalin.

Stalin's face tightened as he read the note. The prospect of open renunciation by Lenin was not a pleasant one; his voice may have become weaker, but it could still be heard in the Party. So Lenin thought he knew what Stalin was up to, did he? Stalin smiled slyly to himself. Well, there was more than one way to accomplish a goal. The surest way to Lenin was through Krupskaya. She had developed a heart condition and was inclined to be very nervous, or, in an emergency, even hysterical. So Lenin was to avoid getting upset for fear it would bring on another, and possibly more serious stroke—

Stalin called Krupskaya on the telephone.

"I have received the note you sent," he told her. "I know that it is your work, not Lenin's. You have poisoned his mind in his illness."

"That's not true," she answered indignantly.

"Yes, it's true," he told her. "You have never been a good Communist. You have held Lenin back and you have held the Party back. You are to blame for many of its failures, perhaps for Lenin's illness, too."

No one had ever questioned her complete devotion to Lenin. She began to cry. "It's all lies," she sobbed into the telephone.

"It's the truth," Stalin said harshly. In the coarsest of terms he went on and on, heaping insults on her. Finally becoming hysterical, she hung up. Stalin leaned back, smiling. "We'll see how Lenin stands that," he said to himself.

But Krupskaya's devotion was greater than he estimated. Instead of going to Lenin, she went to Kamenev and told him the story, asking him to protect her against Stalin.

A weak man to begin with, Kamenev was no match for Stalin. He went to demand an explanation; he came away a member of the conspiracy to seize power, along with Stalin and Zinoviev, when Lenin died. And it would not be long before that happened, Stalin promised him. The net around Lenin was closing tighter and tighter. Stalin had replaced the head of the Cheka with his own man so that he now received daily reports from them on the happenings at Gorki.

One of the doctors attending Lenin was in his pay. It was at best only a question of time.

Still disturbed over the Georgian affair, Lenin had sent Trotsky to investigate.

"It's true," Trotsky reported back grimly. "The worst of the rumors were absolutely correct."

Lenin lay quietly for a moment. "It is grounds for expulsion from the Party," he said, watching Trotsky closely. "It is all the reason we need to get rid of Stalin once and for all."

Trotsky looked out the window, over the rolling fields and the trees. "It would not be so easy as that now," he said. "He has much influence in the Party, people who will follow him regardless of what he has done."

"I see," Lenin answered, thinking Trotsky was afraid to do it, afraid of what would happen. "We will wait then," he said aloud. "Soon I will be better and I will do it myself."

Then he learned of Stalin's attack on Krupskaya. In a fury, he dictated a note and had it delivered.

Dear Comrade Stalin!

You permitted yourself a rude summons of my wife to the telephone and you went on to reprimand her rudely. . . . I have no intention of forgetting so easily something which has been done against me and I do not have to stress that I consider anything done against my wife as done against me. I am therefore asking you to weigh carefully whether you agree to retract your words and apologize, or whether you prefer the severance of relations between us.

Sincerely, Lenin

Two days later, he had another stroke, the most severe yet.

"He has only a few days to live," the doctors said gravely. "Already his right side is completely paralyzed, the left partially. He cannot speak at all. It is the end."

Again, he surprised them. It was almost as though he refused to die, as though he could not give up the struggle.

For two months he hovered between life and death and then he began to recover. Krupskaya worked with him, helping him regain the power of speech. His sister Maria served almost as his right arm. By fall, he was up again, using a cane, dragging his right foot, but able to understand, to talk a little, to think.

In the meantime, Stalin continued his struggle for power. Only two men stood between him and his goal: Lenin and Trotsky. Lenin lay fighting for his life at Gorki; Trotsky must also be removed. At the Thirteenth Party Congress in January, he fired the opening round of the new attack.

"Trotsky has refused to accept the discipline of the Party," he told the assembled delegates. "He has encouraged the intellectuals against us and has undermined our position." He went on to list Trotsky's "crimes" against the Party, in effect, accusing him of high treason. When he walked down from the dais, his eyes held a look of triumph. Any supporters that Trotsky had in the Party would have to think carefully now—did they really want to be on the side of a suspected traitor?

Furthermore, there was no possibility of an answering attack from Trotsky. A few days before, he had mysteriously fallen ill of an ailment the doctors had been unable to diagnose and had been sent to the south of Russia for his health.

The battle lines were drawn; it was time for the final scene to be played. On January 21, three days after the meeting adjourned, Lenin suffered his last attack.

He had gone to bed the night before in good spirits. The doctors were now predicting a full recovery in a few more months and, to look at him, one could easily believe the medical reports. When the maid came to awake him that morning, he seemed just as usual except that he refused breakfast, returning to bed instead. He stayed there all morning, with Maria and Krupskaya checking on him periodically.

At lunch, he ate only a few bites, then returned to bed. One unusual circumstance was to bother them later—the incessant ringing of the telephone. All day, members of the Central Committee, the Cheka, and other organizations kept calling to ask about his health. It was peculiar, since the reports about him had been so good lately, but in their concern for him, they all answered rather absently and it was only later that they began to wonder about it. Had someone known he would suffer an attack that day? If so, who? And how had they known or guessed? They were never to discover the answer.

Around six in the evening there was a change in his breathing and the doctor on duty was called to his bedside. A few minutes later, convulsions shook him with such force that his body actually was lifted from one side of the bed to the other. At 6:50 P.M., he was dead.

It was eleven the next morning before the doctors were allowed to begin the autopsy, although ordinarily it is performed as soon after death as possible. Their report was as expected: he had suffered a recent stroke, there was brain damage.

It was the next day, too, before the public was informed. Trotsky, on a train to the south, was notified by a telegram signed with Stalin's name. He wired back immediately that he was returning. Stalin replied with instructions not to since the funeral would be held before he could arrive. Trotsky continued his journey, still weak from his own illness, filled with grief over the death of the man who had been not only his leader but his friend.

On January 23, Lenin's body was carried in a red coffin to the railroad station to be transported to Moscow. The twenty miles between there and Gorki were lined with people who stood silently as the train passed.

In Moscow, soldiers stood shoulder to shoulder along the street from the depot to the House of Trade Unions where the body was placed on a catafalque. Outside, thousands stood in line in the worst storm Moscow had seen in years. The temperature stayed at twenty degrees below zero while winds of gale force whipped to shreds the black-banded red flags that hung from every window. The sky was somber and threatening. In the thick snow outside, people tried to light bonfires as they waited, to give them some relief from the terrible cold. Many fainted and had to be carried away in ambulances but still they came, from all over Russia.

Sometimes, during the four days he lay in state, the crowd outside sang the old revolutionary songs, sang them softly and slowly, almost like funeral hymns. Inside, members of the Central Committee and the Council of Commissars stood guard at the four corners of the platform, changing shifts every ten minutes.

Only Krupskaya stayed. At first glance, she might have seemed a corpse, too, so immobile, so still, almost like a statue. Others shed tears or wailed; she sat alone, frozen in her grief, unable to express anything. Before her lay her husband, a red blanket covering everything but his head which rested on a snow-white pillow. The loss she felt was too great for words, too deep for tears.

On January 27, the storm suddenly lifted, leaving the skies clear for the first time in days. During the night, the doors had finally been closed and the body placed in a red-draped casket. In the morning, it was moved to Red Square, in front of the Kremlin. There, throughout the long day, party officials gave eulogies, performed the last rites for their leader. At four, by prearrangement, everything in Moscow that could make a noise was sounded, horns, sirens, steam whistles, guns, everything. At the end of three minutes, it was over. Lenin was dead, the funeral was ended, the body taken to a special mausoleum built for that purpose.

But it was just the beginning for Joseph Stalin. Only Lenin and Trotsky had stood in his way; now Lenin was no more. Had he been instrumental in his death? Ugly rumors said so; many believed that he had had him poisoned, that there had been no "strokes" at all. There were many peculiar circumstances surrounding Lenin's illness that lent weight to the rumors. But no one could prove it; no one could do more than have suspicions. Only one thing was sure: Stalin had needed him out of the way and now he was. There remained only Trotsky.

★ ELEVEN

SPRING HAD TURNED THE COUNTRYSIDE TO GREEN AND GOLD when Krupskaya began recovering from her grief. There had been some changes made, she noted. No big changes, just small ones. For one thing, the town of Petrograd, the ex-capital built by Peter the Great and first called St. Petersburg, had been renamed Leningrad in honor of the fallen Communist leader. And Tsaritsyn had been retitled Stalingrad. That was odd—unless one remembered that Tsaritsyn had been the town where Stalin had, in his own eyes, suffered such humiliation at Trotsky's hands and that the motion to change its name had been made by one of his henchmen. It would have seemed odd, that is, had anyone given it some thought.

But no one did. Stalin was looked upon as one of the unsung Party faithfuls, those men who do the work but share little of the glory. As yet, no one knew that by using his office as General Secretary, he had been able to appoint his own supporters to positions of power in all the local Party units. And since the local units elected the higher officers, that meant he had control of practically every office in the Party, as well as the government. But he had worked quietly, behind the scenes, and no one knew yet just how widespread his power was.

Trotsky was beginning to have suspicions. He had watched him narrowly at one of the Party meetings.

"Stalin will become dictator of Russia," he said to a friend standing nearby.

"Stalin?" the other asked in amazement. "But he's a nothing, a colorless nobody!"

Krupskaya was beginning to notice, too. And in her hands lay the weapon that might defeat him—the Last Testament that Lenin had entrusted to her, the document that only she and the secretary knew about. It was the kind of political dynamite that could blow the detested Stalin right out of the Kremlin.

She sought out a few of Lenin's closest supporters on the Central Committee. "I have a paper," she said in her shy, hesitant way. "Lenin wanted it read to the Party." She unfolded it carefully and handed it to one of them.

He raised his eyebrows questioningly and took it from her. As he skimmed over it, his face paled and he handed it quickly to the next man. When they had all finished, they gave it back to her silently.

"It would be very dangerous," one of them said uneasily.

"It was Lenin's wish," she insisted stubbornly.

Despite their reluctance, it was finally agreed that the paper would be read to the Central Committee prior to the general meeting of the Party and they would decide whether or not it should be read to the Party as a whole.

Stalin sat on the steps of the rostrum while it was read. All the damning words were there.

"Comrade Stalin . . . immeasurable power . . . I am not sure . . . sufficient caution . . . too coarse . . . someone more loyal."

As though from the grave itself, the members listened to Lenin's own words. Could they ignore the advice of Lenin, their leader? No—more than a leader, a hero, an idol, almost, since his death four short months ago, a god.

Stalin kept his head bowed, his eyes half-closed, his face pale with embarrassment and strain. Some of that embarrassment was reflected in the audience; they were completely silent, careful not to look at the small, miserable figure huddled on the steps.

The last words were still echoing in the hall when Zinoviev jumped to his feet and rushed to the speaker's platform.

"Comrades, every word of Lenin's is law to us," he said in a deep, serious voice, "but we are happy to say that in one

point, Lenin's fears have proved groundless. I have in mind
the point about our General Secretary. You have all seen
how well everything has been going. Like myself, you will be
happy to say that Lenin's fears were without foundation."

The members looked around at each other; here and there,
one man nodded to another. Stalin had been doing a good
job, they seemed to be saying. Zinoviev took his seat and
Kamenev walked to the platform.

"We must keep Joseph Stalin in office," he told them,
"for our own sakes; Stalin works only for the good of the
Party." He hesitated and looked around. This time there
were more nods, even a few smiles. "And if we do," he went
on, "we must not disturb the Party by reading this paper
at the meeting."

"No, no! It must be read!" Krupskaya called from the side
of the hall. The audience ignored her. The other voice that
might have been raised was strangely silent. Leon Trotsky,
too proud to speak when he stood to gain personally by it,
kept quiet, betraying his disgust with the scene only by his
facial expression.

Again Zinoviev was on his feet. "I move that the Testament not be made public," he said in a clear, ringing voice.

There were sighs of relief when the vote was taken. The
motion passed, forty to ten. For Stalin, the crisis had been
averted.

He had every reason now to be smug. After all, he had
won over the great Lenin himself; who else was there who
might defeat him? Certainly not the weaklings Kamenev
and Zinoviev.

For their part, they were too busy congratulating each
other to worry about him.

"A good day's work," Zinoviev said, leaning back in his
chair. "Stalin is much less dangerous than Trotsky would
have been."

"Yes," Kamenev agreed. They were both thinking the
same thing: Trotsky with his dynamic personality, his intelligence, the control of the army, and above all, his ambition,
had been much more of a threat than Stalin would ever be.

"Stalin is not well known outside the Party itself," Zinoviev added after a moment. He contrasted it mentally with his own popularity. No, Stalin would not be a threat when it came time for him, Zinoviev, to take over the leadership.

"That's right," Kamenev said. "He's a simple man. Maybe a little too simple," he added with a smile, tapping his temple and grimacing to indicate that Stalin was not too bright. Quite a contrast to himself, he thought, but that would make him that much easier to dispose of when the time came for him, Kamenev, to take over.

They smiled at each other.

Working with Stalin, they found yet another way to discredit Trotsky. Searching through the early writings of both Lenin and Trotsky, they ferreted out all the points of difference between them and publicized them, making it sound as though they had been miles apart on every question.

Trotsky began publishing his own pamphlets, pointing out that both Zinoviev and Kamenev had been against the Bolshevik overthrow of the Provisional Government. They replied in kind. The war of nerves had begun in earnest.

Only Stalin seemed unaffected by the situation. He went quietly along, stolidly smoking his pipe at the meetings, adding a word here, further seeds of doubt there.

"I am concerned about Trotsky," he confided casually to some of the Party members. He shook his head slowly, a frown on his face. "He is creating dissension in the Party, breaking it into factions."

Kamenev and Zinoviev urged him to take more drastic action against Trotsky.

"No," he said firmly. "You chop off one head today, another one tomorrow, still another the day after—what in the end will be left of the Party?" He surveyed them shrewdly. "My concern is only for the Party," he reassured them.

The gulf between the two points of view, Stalin's and Trotsky's, did seem to be widening daily. Trotsky wanted to hold the Communists to their original position—that of sponsoring a world-wide socialist revolution. Stalin believed that they must first concentrate on establishing themselves

irrevocably in Russia. Real communism must be reintro-
duced to the peasants; Russia's industry must be built up
until she could exist independently of the world community.
Then perhaps, he shrugged, they would worry about the rest
of the world.

Conveniently, Trotsky's health again became bad and once
more, it was a mysterious ailment the doctors could not
diagnose. It was too bad, Stalin said, but he would have to
be replaced as Commissar of War.

Trotsky scarcely had time to protest his abrupt dismissal
before he was again taken ill, this time seriously. He was
taken to the Kremlin Clinic, where he did not seem to
improve.

With consciousness ebbing and returning, he remembered
Lenin's last illness. He had never really believed in the
strokes; he had always believed that Stalin had in some way
managed to poison Lenin. "And now I'm next," he thought
suddenly. "Am I to lie here and die, another victim of
Stalin's cunning?"

Summoning the last of his strength, he called the attendant. "I want you to find a friend of mine and tell him
I am here," he said. "Tell him to come immediately; I am
dying."

The attendant stared back at him with frightened eyes.
"Go!" Trotsky commanded. He watched until the young
man was safely through the door, then lay back exhausted
on his pillow. He held on to his fast-fading strength until
the attendant returned with the friend. Briefly and privately,
he told him his suspicions. The friend promptly arranged
for his removal from the clinic and moved him to the
Crimea, a resort on the Black Sea in southern Russia, where
he began to recover.

Behind the scenes, Stalin could now permit himself a
slight smile as he puffed on the ever-present pipe. One of
his biggest fears had been that Trotsky might use his popularity and position of power in the army to stage a coup
d'état and overthrow the existing government. Now he was
safely out of contact with the army, removed from his post,

safely out of the picture altogether. Zinoviev and Kamenev, who had proved themselves to be useful in disposing of Trotsky, were no longer needed.

But there was no hurry. He waited until the Fourteenth Party Congress in 1925. There he fired his opening gun.

"We must beware of traitors," he told the delegates, "those who would dissipate our strength by dividing it, men like Zinoviev and Kamenev who try to split the Party into factions."

It was a grave sin to the Communists. They all believed that only one party could exist successfully in a Communist state and that party, of course, must be the Communist Party. There were excited whisperings in the audience and Stalin went on to other topics. It was enough for a beginning. There was one more detail to be seen to: the Cheka, or secret police, must be brought firmly under his control before he proceeded. Within a short while, the Chief of Cheka met an untimely death and was replaced by Stalin's old friend, Klim Voroshilov. He could now turn his attention back to Zinoviev, Kamenev and Trotsky, who had recovered and was making critical speeches to workers' groups around Moscow.

Stalin again raised the cry of "factionalism." This time he added other accusations: Zinoviev and Kamenev were the "deserters" and "strike-breakers of the revolution," he said. These were the same charges he had defended them against when Trotsky made them; but he had needed the two of them then and he did not need them now.

His opposition, together with the previous attacks by Trotsky, was enough. Both Zinoviev and Kamenev found themselves avoided by other Party members. And both were frightened.

It was in fright that they first approached Trotsky. Perhaps the three of them working together could defeat the evil Stalin, they suggested. After all, they still had influence in the Party, they believed. They pointed out to Trotsky that he stood in as much danger as they.

"You think Stalin is busy figuring out how to reply to your

arguments," Kamenev said. "Nothing of the sort. He is try-ing to find a way to liquidate you without getting caught."

"He would have put an end to you as long ago as 1924," Zinoviev added, "if he hadn't been afraid of retaliation."

But what could they do against the power of Stalin? They were old revolutionaries; they knew a thing or two about behind-the-scenes maneuverings. Zinoviev was still head of the Leningrad Soviet. Working through it, they began to organize small groups of anti-Stalinists. Meetings were held, pamphlets printed and circulated, plans laid.

Some of the younger members, lacking the patience of the old veterans, began distributing the pamphlets openly. They were promptly arrested and deported to Siberia, except for two who were armed. They were shot. It was a warning and the conspirators understood it.

Both Kamenev and Zinoviev urged Trotsky to do as they had done: write a letter and put it into safe hands with in-structions that it be made public in the event they should die suddenly. It was obvious to all of them that the present situation could not continue much longer.

To men steeled for a sudden attack, Stalin appeared to move with maddening slowness. In February, 1926, Zinoviev was removed as head of the Leningrad Soviet. But it was not until July that the real blow fell.

At a meeting of the Party's Central Committee, one of Stalin's lieutenants reported the uncovering of a plot within the Kremlin itself, a plot designed to take the Kremlin by storm and massacre the Politburo. Seven men had been shot, he said, and a secret cache of arms uncovered. Trotsky, Zinoviev and Kamenev were asked for explanations.

Zinoviev and Kamenev denied any knowledge of it, quietly and completely. It was Trotsky, the usually calm and self-possessed, who lost his temper. He recognized the scheme for what it actually was: an attempt to get rid of the three of them.

"There's the real conspirator against the Communist Party!" he shouted from the rostrum, pointing at Stalin.

His face contorted with anger, Stalin stood up and shook

his fist at Trotsky; then, with a supreme effort, turned his back and walked out of the hall.

There were few people there who did not know that Trotsky had just signed his own death warrant. As the door closed behind Stalin, one of the spectators whispered to the man next to him, "Stalin would not forgive his own grandchildren for that."

Nor would he forgive Trotsky. The Central Committee, filled with Stalin's supporters, contented themselves, this time, with expelling Zinoviev from his positions as a member of the Politburo and head of the Communist international organization; but a few months later, Trotsky and Kamenev fell victim to a similar fate.

They had tried to forestall it. Two weeks earlier, the three of them had signed statements admitting that they were guilty of breaking Party rules by disagreeing publicly with Party policy and promising to abstain from such activities in the future. At the Central Committee meeting, Trotsky had tried to speak but his voice had been drowned in a sea of catcalls and jeers. The Committee was Stalin's; the members were merely puppets who moved when he pulled the strings.

But Trotsky still had some influence with the people and with the rank-and-file Party membership; he was still the living symbol of the military victory the Bolsheviks had achieved. It was still necessary for Stalin to move carefully; there was always the possibility of an uprising should anything happen to Trotsky before he was completely discredited. For the present, Stalin contented himself with publicly ridiculing the three of them, calling attention to the bitter things they had said about each other in the past.

It was a year before he was sufficiently self-confident to make his next move: the expulsion of Trotsky and Kamenev from the Central Committee. But it was not enough. They were still Party members, still potentially dangerous should they find a way to attract support for their cause. Some way must be found to get rid of them permanently. Still he could not move openly against them; he must wait for them to provide him with an excuse.

Two weeks later, on November 7, 1927, they did. Demonstrations had been planned to celebrate the tenth anniversary of the Bolshevik takeover, parades and speeches in both Moscow and Leningrad. Tired of doing little in their own defense, Trotsky and Zinoviev decided to use the celebrations to dramatize their cause.

On the appointed day, they organized their followers to march on streets parallel to the main parade, carrying banners and placards which bore their own slogans instead of reflecting the government policy as the others did. The marches were peaceful and without incident but they were enough.

Five days later the Central Committee met and voted to expel the three of them from the Party. Now all that remained was to have the general Party Congress, which would convene a month later, approve the action.

There had been no one in the Central Committee who wished to risk his own future to defend Trotsky, Zinoviev and Kamenev; nor was there anyone in the Party Congress who would do so. Stalin had long ago learned the secret of absolute control. At every Party meeting, specially trusted henchmen of Stalin's sat in the audience, taking note of each speaker and, afterward, researching his past life to find grounds for blackmail or intimidation.

Only one man had tried to register a protest against the carefully stage-managed proceedings. Adolph Joffe, another of the founders of Bolshevisim and Lenin's first ambassador to Germany, had written a letter to Trotsky, telling him that he was committing suicide as a protest against Stalinism; then he had shot himself.

The contents of the letter had become known to the general public through secretly printed and distributed pamphlets and, the day of the funeral, huge crowds had turned out to pay honor to the old revolutionary. Trotsky, pale and troubled, had followed the coffin to its final resting place. At the gates of the cemetery, the OGPU, the new name for the Cheka, held the crowds back, allowing only a few of Joffe's friends and his family through.

The crowd pressed against the fence and watched the last rites. As the red-draped casket was lowered into the grave, there was a spontaneous roar: "Down with Stalin!" The OGPU chief jumped the fence, and the guards immediately raised their rifles.

Trotsky raised his bent head slowly and looked out at the crowd. He lifted both arms toward the sky, his grief-stricken face presenting his plea for silence more eloquently than words. The crowd hushed immediately and Trotsky turned back to the grave, his shoulders slumped, his face haggard, a beaten man, a man without hope.

Joffe's death had no effect on the Party Congress which now demanded that Trotsky, Zinoviev and Kamenev denounce and renounce their own views.

Kamenev, badly frightened, argued from the platform that such demands contradicted the traditions of Bolshevism. The swarm of delegates shouted him down angrily, then proceeded to vote for the expulsion of the three of them from the Party.

Only Trotsky came through the ordeal without shame. Both Zinoviev and Kamenev bowed to Stalin's steamroller tactics and abandoned their differences of opinion with him; both begged the delegates for reinstatement in the Party. Trotsky, clutching to him the few shreds of dignity that Stalin had left, refused, and the delegates voted that he be exiled to Siberia. As for Zinoviev and Kamenev, the delegates shrugged, that could be left to Stalin to take care of. It was voted that he should make the decision about taking them back into the Party.

Joffe's funeral had proved one thing: Trotsky was still not entirely without influence. The Politburo, fearing that if some accident occurred to him an uprising might take place, handled his arrest and deportation themselves. Special guards were posted around his apartment until arrangements had been made to transport him to Alma Ata, in south central Russia.

For Leon Trotsky, his wife and two sons, the next month was like an eternity. Guards watched their every move; no visitors were allowed in without permission from the Politburo and the OGPU; they were not allowed to go out. Yet when the time came to go, Trotsky was not ready to give up.

Early on the morning of January 16, 1928, the guards told the family to pack; their train would leave later that day. Trotsky went into his room, as though to get ready, and locked the door. The guards pleaded, cajoled and threatened. He would not unlock it.

They sent one of their number to the Politburo to ask what they were to do now. The decision was to break down the door if he did not come out when the train was ready to leave.

To lessen the possibility of an uprising, the railroad station and all streets leading to it were cleared. Troops were in evidence everywhere. Machine-gun squads and armored cars were set up at the intersections of all streets approaching the station.

Inside the station, only a few employees and a handful of officials witnessed the scene that followed. A group of OGPU officers entered, their pistols drawn, their eyes darting around the station looking for signs of trouble. Next came a group of men dressed in everyday clothes, carrying what appeared to be a large bundle wrapped in a heavy fur coat.

It was Leon Trotsky, still wearing the pajamas and socks in which he had been surprised when the guards had made their announcement. Now, his hair disheveled, his glasses sitting crookedly on his nose, he was carried through the station, out onto the platform to the waiting train. Behind him trailed his wife, accompanied by Mrs. Joffe and another woman. The younger son, Lyev, ran from one person to another, pleading with them hysterically to help his father. On the platform, the older boy, Sergei, finally breaking under the tension, threw himself on one of the guards and began to beat him wildly with clenched fists. Others came to the guard's rescue, pulled the boy off and pushed him into the train.

Mrs. Joffe and the other woman stood on the platform, weeping softly, as the train began to chug solemnly down the track. It was a long way to Alma Ata; it would be a long trip.

Back in the days when Zinoviev and Kamenev had teamed with Stalin to defeat the man now traveling toward the wastelands of Russia, Stalin had said to them, "There can be no greater pleasure in life than to choose one's enemy, inflict a terrible revenge on him and go quietly to sleep."

As the train hurtled through the frigid Russian night, Zinoviev and Kamenev, still in Moscow, were terrorized over what their fate would be. And Stalin, by his own words, was sleeping peacefully, dreaming pleasant dreams.

★ TWELVE

"Papa! Papa!" A small boy hurtled through the doorway of the cottage, his coattails flying behind him. "There's a truck coming down the road! Filled with soldiers!"

The bearded peasant took another swallow of his soup, avoiding the anxious gaze of his wife from across the table. "So?" he said to the boy. "Your standing up will not bring them sooner. Sit down and eat your soup before it cools."

"But, Papa—"

The peasant looked up at the boy, who promptly removed his cap and slid into his place at the table. The family sat stiff and silent as the sound of a motor came nearer, then stopped. A moment later, a heavy hand knocked at the door. The father rose slowly. On the way to the door, he straightened his back and lifted his head.

"Yes?" he said to the officer who stood outside.

"Yuri Shastinovich?" the officer inquired mechanically.

"Yes."

"You and your family did not report to the collectivized farm last week as you were ordered to do."

The peasant drew a deep breath. "No," he said, "we did not. I told the men who came that we do not believe in collectivized farms. We will stay here on our own land."

"Old man," the officer said with a sneer, "do you not want to obey the orders of our glorious leader Stalin? He says all farmers must report to the collectivized farms, where they will have modern equipment and all the new techniques. That way they can grow more food to feed our workers in the cities."

141

"I will feed them with what I can grow here, on my own farm," the peasant answered stiffly.

"These peasants are so stupid," the officer muttered over his shoulder to his sergeant. "Listen carefully, old man. You must take all your livestock, your supplies and your tools and report immediately to the collective farm. There you will share what you have with the others. At harvest, you and the others will pay part of your grain to the government for the use of the land, part of it to the machine tractor station for the use of the machinery, and the rest will be yours to divide among yourselves. In this way, you will all benefit, do you understand? You will be able to produce more for the workers and you will have more for yourself."

"I will not go," the peasant repeated. "My family and I, we stay on our land."

"But the land does not belong to you—oh, what's the use of talk?" the officer said disgustedly. He turned toward the peasant's wife, who stood across the room, her arm protectively around the boy's shoulders. "Do you have other menfolk around here?"

She swallowed hard and nodded. "A father and a brother," she said. "A little distance to the west."

"Tell them what happens to men who will not go to the collectives," the officer said harshly. He turned quickly on his heel, nodding at the squad of soldiers behind him. As he passed them, a sudden volley of shots rang out. The peasant cried out once and fell. The men turned, loaded back into the truck, and drove away.

The scene was repeated over and over in Russia, in the early 1930s. Sometimes the peasants took refuge in the forests, sometimes they killed their livestock, burned their grain, and reported to the collectives emptyhanded. Occasionally, they fought back, killing a few soldiers, little enough retaliation for several hundred dead peasants. In the end, the result was the same, however; the farms were collectivized over the bitter protest of the peasants. Thousands were deported to Siberia, many put to work in slave labor camps, thousands more were killed.

The collectivization of farms, or combining of the small farms into fewer large ones, was only one facet of Stalin's first Five Year Plan.

"We are fifty to one hundred years behind the advanced countries," Stalin said. "We must make up this lag in ten years. Either we do this or they will crush us."

The Five Year Plans, the first to run from 1928 to 1933, were his program for doing it. Agriculture was to be collectivized, thereby producing more food through the use of modern machinery and techniques and also using fewer workers, who could then move to the cities and go to work in the new factories.

But the hardships brought upon the people by the first Five Year Plan and the far-reaching goals it set, gave rise to much grumbling. Ever fearful of a conspiracy against him, Stalin determined to put an end to it. The members of the Politburo were commanded not to make critical statements. Foreign newsmen were limited to visiting only certain sections of the country. And the relentless war against the peasants continued.

To make up for the failures of the Five Year Plan, to keep its weaknesses from being blamed on the Communists, a series of trials was held. Engineers and technicians accused of sabotaging the plan were tried and found guilty.

Still Stalin was not satisfied. Deep distrust was a part of his nature; was someone working to undermine him in the same way he had worked to undermine Lenin and Trotsky? He did not know; the only way to be sure was to get rid of anyone who might possibly try. In 1934, the stage was set for the strange drama that was to become known as the "Great Terror."

The leader of the Leningrad Soviet, a man named Kerov, was one of those whose personal loyalty to Stalin was questionable. He was too independent, too concerned with the welfare of his own people. On December 1, 1934, Kerov was assassinated. His murderer confessed freely to the crime and was tried in a secret military court.

A month later, Stalin's old enemies, Zinoviev and Kamenev, were dragged from their semiretirement and placed on trial for "the political and moral responsibility" of Kerov's murder. They were the leaders a secret counterrevolutionary group to which the murderer belonged, the prosecution charged. Both were found guilty and Zinoviev received ten years in prison, Kamenev, five. If it was a farce, no one in Russia found it funny, least of all Zinoviev and Kamenev, who were promptly imprisoned.

The OGPU, or secret police, was now combined with the Department of the Interior to form a new and more powerful police organization called the NKVD and its full force was turned upon the Party which had grown from twenty-five thousand in 1917 to three and a half million in 1933. The old Bolsheviks, those who had joined the Party prior to the 1917 revolution, found themselves under constant surveillance, treated like criminals. Then in August, 1936, Zinoviev and Kamenev reappeared on the scene.

The stage was a courtroom in Moscow; the actors, in addition to Zinoviev and Kamenev, fourteen other defendants, the judges of the Supreme Military Tribunal of the Union of Soviet Socialist Republics, a court secretary, Andrei Vishinsky, the prosecutor, and a multitude of guards. There was no jury and no defense counsel. A small audience served as spectators for the drama.

At one end of the room, the prisoners sat on several rows of wooden chairs, their profiles turned to the audience which was separated from them by a low wooden bar. Near the bar stood three tall, armed guards with bayonets fixed on their rifles. At the opposite end, at a small table, sat Vishinsky.

Zinoviev in particular looked bad. The asthma from which he had suffered for a long time was complicated now by heart trouble. His face was swollen and puffy; there were heavy bags under his eyes. Like the other defendants, he sat quietly while the President of the Court established the identity of the prisoners, then had the charges against them read.

Sabotage, treason—those were only a portion of the many

crimes they were accused of committing. There was no surprise on the prisoners' faces, only the reflection of a seeming desire to get it over with, to have done with it. Each of them testified and confessed freely to the charges.

"The Party saw where we were going and warned us," Zinoviev said. "But we did not heed those warnings."

"This is the third time I am facing a proletarian court," Kamenev said. "Twice my life was spared. But there is a limit to the generosity of the people and we have reached that limit."

There was no doubt in the minds of the more knowing spectators that both Zinoviev and Kamenev were working hard to save not themselves, but their families. Each seemed eager to trade any kind of self-abasement for the safety of the relatives they would leave behind them.

There was another defendant at the trial—a silent one, one who could give no testimony for or against himself. It soon became obvious to all that the one who was really on trial was Leon Trotsky, who had now been exiled from Russia altogether, along with Natalia and one of his sons, Lyev, while the other son was forced to remain in Russia. Each defendant implicated Trotsky in all that he did. Stalin might not be able to bring Trotsky into the courtroom, but he could use the courtroom to paint Trotsky as a criminal and assassin in the eyes of the world. Along with him, Lyev was presented as a traitor and a killer.

On the morning of August 22, each defendant was allowed to present a last plea.

"I should like to say a few words to my children," Kamenev said. "No matter what my sentence is, I consider it just. Don't look back. Go forward. Follow Stalin along with the Soviet people." It was almost an open request. "Don't make trouble if they execute me," he was saying. "Play it safe, save your own lives."

At two-thirty in the morning, August 24, the judges returned with their verdict. All of the defendants were sentenced to death by shooting. None showed surprise; all seemed to be waiting for the judge to go on, as though they expected him to commute the sentences. Surely they had received some bargain in return for their eager performance on the stands, their cooperation in reviling Leon Trotsky. But the judge was silent and the prisoners were led from the courtroom. The newspapers carried the story the following day reporting that all sixteen had been executed.

Many Russians breathed a sigh of relief when the grim, ugly business was over. But they were premature; the trial of Zinoviev and Kamenev was not the end, it was only the beginning. A month later, Yagoda, the head of the NKVD, was replaced by a man named Yeshov who richly deserved his reputation as an "ignorant, sadistic hangman," and the trials began anew.

Before they ended in 1938, tens of thousands of Russians in all walks of life had been arrested, tried and convicted. Red Army generals, high government officials, newspaper editors, ambassadors, the judges from the first trials, even the ex-chief of the NKVD were included in the mass purge. The walls of the prisons and the prison trains were covered with scratches—"Why?" "What for?" "Why are we here?"— but in the courtroom, all behaved the same way. They confessed to the most outrageous crimes: plots on Stalin's life, treason, interfering with the Five Year Plans, murder. And one other common thread ran through the trials: many of the defendants vowed that they belonged to a secret conspiracy headed by Leon Trotsky, a conspiracy that variously planned Stalin's assassination, the bombing of the Kremlin, turning Russia over to the Germans under Hitler, and reestablishing capitalism in the U.S.S.R. Trotsky, along with the others, was found guilty and sentenced to death.

But Trotsky, unlike Stalin's other victims, was outside his reach. He and Natalia had been offered political asylum by the Mexican government and, in 1937, the two of them landed at Tampico, where they were met by the president's special train and whisked away to Mexico City. Diego Rivera, the famous Mexican painter, and one of the founders of the Mexican Communist Party, offered them his famous "Blue

House," and for the first time in many years they settled down with a feeling of safety and security.

The years between had been difficult ones. Most of their family had been left behind in Russia, at Stalin's insistence. Nina and Zina, his two daughters, had died; Sergei, the older son, was reported to have been arrested in Siberia and charged with the mass poisoning of factory workers under his father's direction. Only two weeks after his landing in Mexico, the news from Russia told of his being accused by Vishinsky, the prosecutor in the Moscow purge trials, of organizing and directing industrial sabotage, catastrophes in coal mines, factories and railroads, and attempts to murder the entire Politburo. Then the phone calls began, anonymous calls which threatened his life and his family's safety. Lyev, who had stayed behind in Paris to supervise the publications put out by Trotsky and his followers, was being shadowed wherever he went.

Then Lyev published a statement in the Paris newspapers that he was in good health and was not entertaining any thoughts of suicide, and if he were to die suddenly, it would be at Stalin's hand. It was the breaking point for Trotsky. He appealed to the League of Nations for a chance to tell his story to the Commission on Political Terrorism. Nothing happened. He continued his appeals, wrote voluminously and vehemently, and finally, a Joint Commission of Inquiry was formed to investigate the matter.

John Dewey, the famous American educator and non-Communist, was appointed chairman of the commission, which included French, British, American and Czechoslovakian members. Under his leadership, the commission made a thorough investigation of each charge made against Trotsky in the course of the Moscow trials. They spent endless hours sifting the evidence and interviewing Trotsky himself. Several months later, they presented their verdict.

"On the basis of all the evidence . . . we find the trials of August, 1936, and January, 1937, were frame-ups . . . we find Leon Trotsky . . . not guilty."

Trotsky had been vindicated in the eyes of the world but he felt sure that this would not save him from Stalin's vengeance. Nor could it save Lyev. Then news reached the Trotskys in Mexico of Lyev's death. He had been operated on for appendicitis at a small private hospital in Paris. He had recovered and was doing well for a few days, then there was a mysterious relapse with attacks of pain and finally, unconsciousness and death.

Trotsky immediately made arrangements for Seva, the grandson who had been living with Lyev in Paris, to join him and Natalia in Mexico. The only other relatives left were in Russia, cut off from them as completely as if they, too, were dead. Trotsky moved Seva, Natalia and himself into a walled and fortified villa at Coyoacan.

"Why?" the rest of the world wondered. Why the trials, why the persecution of Trotsky? The answers lay in Stalin's mind and no one could see that completely. Trotsky was a threat to Stalin—he had established the Fourth International, a Communist group which rivaled Stalin's own organization for membership; his attacks on Stalin were published and read throughout the world—and he was an old enemy.

The others? The tens of thousands who died in the purges? Many were old Bolsheviks, those who had been with the Party in the early days, who had known Lenin and the early dreams. Not one of those who had been prominent in the Party in the early years survived the purges. It was as though Stalin was determined to erase every possibility of opposition to himself or his policies, along with everyone who had known too much about his earlier career.

The technicians and engineers who were tried were charged with causing the hardships and mistakes in the Five Year Plans. Even Yeshov, the hangman, finally fell victim to the terrorism he had helped to create. He was replaced by Lavrenty Beria, a Georgian of peasant background, and committed to a lunatic asylum in order to avoid the scandal of an open trial, since his predecessor had only recently been tried and executed. Several months later, his body was found hanging from an aspen tree, a sign, "I am just filthy carrion," tied around his neck.

Estimates of the total convicted in the trials, either imprisoned or liquidated, ran from seven to fifteen millions. To the outside world, it seemed that Stalin was preparing to build himself into a god instead of just a leader. When he announced the end of the trials in 1938, there was no one left in Russia who could oppose him, no mistake which could be blamed on him. The history books were rewritten to exclude Leon Trotsky's name and give Stalin more credit for the 1917 revolution. All textbooks on every level were filled with references to "Our Great Leader Stalin." Pictures of him were placed in all public buildings, statues erected in the town squares.

But the outside world had little time to concern itself with what was going on in Russia. There were too many other events occurring, events which appeared to be more pressing, such as Adolf Hitler's seizure of territory in Europe. Under the second and third Five Year Plans, Russia's industry had grown tremendously, but it was known to be still weak and there were doubts that it could support a modern army. Furthermore, the Great Terror had weakened the Red Army considerably by the execution of scores of its leaders. The outside world was concerned with Hitler, not Stalin.

Stalin was concerned with Hitler, too. His plans for conquest of Poland were well known and Poland was all that stood between Russia and Germany. There were reports from Russian agents in Germany that Hitler also had his eye on the Ukraine, the southern agricultural region so important to Russia.

In the early years of Stalin's rule, Germany and Russia had been friendly despite their differences in political philosophy. Both of them had been outcast nations in the world community and, in 1933, had signed a neutrality treaty at a time when Russian diplomats were being insulted and humiliated in every other capital of the world. However, in 1936, three short years later, Germany had signed a pact with Japan, pledging opposition to the international Communist organization and to all nations who supported it. Russia's name was not mentioned specifically, but there could be no doubt that it was the target of the agreement. All in all, Stalin felt, it was time to do something. He still expected the former Allies of World War I, France, Great Britain and the United States, to make attempts to overthrow him. An agreement with Germany would help protect him from them and from Germany itself.

His first step was to appoint Vyacheslav Molotov as Minister of Foreign Affairs. Molotov, a quiet, colorless man, had been a long-time associate of Stalin's and his loyalty was unquestioned. He had met Stalin first in 1912 when both had worked on the Bolshevik newspaper, *Pravda*, and had been his faithful lieutenant ever since. He had become a member of the Politburo in 1921, despite the fact that Lenin had little respect for him and referred to him as "an incurable dumbbell" and "the best file clerk in Russia." He was not a brilliant negotiator but he was a shrewd and capable one.

The former head of the Moscow Party organization, Nikita Khrushchev, was sent to the Ukraine, assigned to purge any Party leaders of questionable loyalty. If the Germans did have designs on that area, there was to be no one who might cooperate with them. Khrushchev, a former coal miner who had acquired his education in night school and proved himself to be efficient and reliable in carrying out difficult jobs, was highly successful and, in 1939, was made a member of the Politburo.

In Berlin, Molotov was proving himself equally successful. On August 19, a trade agreement was signed that would bring Russia some of the machinery and military supplies she so badly needed in return for raw materials and grain. A few days later, the Ribbentrop-Molotov Pact was signed. It promised that Germany and Russia would each observe "benevolent neutrality" in case the other went to war.

When the rest of Europe went to war only a few days later, Stalin was overjoyed. The capitalist world was now caught up in a war which promised to be long and exhausting. Russia would have plenty of time to build up her armed forces, increase her territory at the expense of her neighbors, and, when the war was over, and the capitalist countries weak and helpless, effect the world revolution which would make communism supreme.

When Hitler took western Poland on the first of September, Stalin waited only a few days to annex the eastern portion and add it to the Russian states of the Ukraine and Byelorussia. Then, while Hitler kept the rest of Europe busy, Stalin forced the tiny Baltic states of Estonia, Latvia and Lithuania to sign "mutual assistance" treaties and to admit Russian troops to "protect" them. Overwhelmed by his success, he delivered a summons to Finland, the small state to the north which had been an autonomous Russian province prior to the 1917 treaty of Brest-Litovsk, to cede to Russia territory near Leningrad in exchange for some land in the interior. The independent Finns didn't reply.

On November 29, 1939, Stalin struck. Unexpectedly, the Finns put up a fierce resistance and thoroughly taxed the strength of the Red Army before finally being forced into a surrender the following March. Stalin took the city of Vyborg and a naval base as a part of the peace terms. A short time later, he sent an ultimatum to the Baltic states, demanding that they install Communist governments. With no allies to come to their aid, they had no recourse but to do as he asked.

By early summer, 1940, he could sit back and smilingly contemplate his gains. He had recovered almost all the territory Russia had lost in 1917; he had enlarged his empire and brought it under his complete control. The capitalist world was engaged in a devastating war in which he would be only a spectator. One flaw remained in the picture: Leon Trotsky, who was still writing his furious attacks from Mexico and still gathering supporters for his Fourth International.

On August 21, 1940, Leon Trotsky was dead, murdered by a strange assailant called Frank Jacson, whose true iden-

tity was not finally established until ten years later as Jaime
Ramón Hernández del Rio Mercader. But even while the
world puzzled over who he was, his mother, Caridad, a long-
time Communist, was taken to Moscow and presented to
Stalin. In a secret ceremony, she accepted the Order of
Lenin, the highest decoration Stalin could give, for herself
and her son.

Trotsky's voice was finally stilled. His last enemy laid to
rest, Stalin could sleep easy.

Not according to the British and American ambassadors
in Moscow, however.

"We have reason to believe that Hitler is preparing an
attack on Russia," they told Stalin in a secret conference.

Stalin lifted suspicious eyebrows. "When is this attack to
take place?" he asked.

The two ambassadors looked at each other. The disbelief
in his voice was obvious.

"In the spring, according to our information," the American answered.

"Do you think it's true?" one of Stalin's aides asked him
after the two had left.

He sat staring at the door through which they had departed. "Who knows?" he answered, shrugging slightly. It
could be a ruse, he thought to himself. The British and the
Americans would like nothing better than to involve him in
the war, particularly on Britain's side.

"What about our trade agreement with Germany?" the
aide persisted. "The grain and raw materials we have promised them?"

"We will deliver them," Stalin answered. If it came to a
choice, he would trust Hitler before he would trust the
British and Americans.

He paced up and down the floor for a few moments, lost
in thought, then stopped. "We will do one thing, though. We
will build up the army a little."

"Then you believe them?" the aide asked.

Stalin hesitated. "No," he said finally, "but the army needs
building up anyway."

In search of still more security, Stalin signed a treaty in the spring of 1941 with Japan who had joined Italy and Germany as a member of the Axis powers. It was similar to the treaty he had with Germany. Inside the Kremlin, he could lean back and relax. Now he was protected on both sides.

Then on June 22, 1941, the German army wheeled across the Neiman River, through Poland, in a three-pronged attack aimed at Leningrad, Moscow and the Ukraine. The meager defense units at the border were swept aside and the mechanized armies of Hitler's Wehrmacht, or war machine, rolled in at surprising speed.

★ THIRTEEN

"NO ONE HAS BEEN A MORE CONSTANT OPPONENT OF COMMU-
nism than I have. . . . But . . . any man or nation who
fights on against Nazidom . . . will have our aid."

It was Prime Minister Winston Churchill speaking from
Great Britain and his words were the signal for Allied ships
to begin carrying arms, munitions, machinery, supplies of
every kind into Russian ports. The United States offered
immediate aid, too, through the Lend-Lease plan by which
it had been helping Great Britain.

"Let them," Hitler said. "They will find it takes time for
the supplies to reach the front lines and by then," he extended his open hand, "we will hold Russia *there.*" He
closed his hand suddenly into a fist, smiling wildly around
the conference table at his aides.

"But, mein Führer," one of them said with a frown, "the
Russian winter—"

"The Russian winter will find us in possession of the
Russian country," Hitler said emphatically.

For a time, it appeared he was right. By December, when
the United States officially entered the war as a result of the
Japanese sneak attack on Pearl Harbor in Hawaii, Leningrad was encircled by the Nazis, Moscow was threatened,
and the Ukraine was under partial control. There the
Wehrmacht stalled.

"What do you mean, you are stalled?" Hitler ranted to
one of his eastern commanders. "I command you to keep
moving."

"Remember the weather, mein Führer," the commander
pleaded. "Constant snow, below-zero temperatures. It is the

154

worst winter in living memory. Our troops are not used to it. And the Russians burned the ground behind them when they moved east. We were able to seize little food. We are forced to bring supplies all the way from Germany itself."

"Then do so," Hitler demanded again, "but keep moving. I must have Russia, do you understand?"

"There are the peasants, too," the commander went on.

"The peasants? Do you not even know how to defeat the civilian population? Are we so soft and weak we quail before ignorant peasants?" Hitler asked harshly.

"No, mein Führer," the commander answered in a strained voice. "We have shot millions of them and deported more millions to the slave labor camps but still they fight on."

"Do they have tanks and planes?" Hitler spat out contemptuously. "How is it they can stop the Wehrmacht?"

"They harass our supply lines and attack our rear. They come like ghosts out of the blinding snow and before we've scarcely seen them, they have done their damage and disappeared again," the commander replied, brushing a weary hand across his eyes.

"Do they love the Communists so much?" Hitler asked with a frown.

"No," the commander answered. "They love the land. And they hate us."

So the peasants fought on. What machinery could be moved had been taken east of the Urals, the mountain range which divides Russia north and south, and the skilled workers went with it. The war became a contest between the Wehrmacht and the hardy peasants as the Red Army retreated eastward across the country. Even when the peasants' clothes became rags, when they were threatened with starvation, when they were on the verge of freezing to death from lack of fuel, they fought fiercely on. Leningrad, the city Peter the Great had built and Lenin had conquered, held out for months against the circle of Nazis and the total lack of any kind of new supplies or reinforcements.

In the spring, the Russians were able to mount a counteroffensive but the result was not too satisfactory. The Germans gave a little ground in central Russia, took a little in the southern sector.

"We must have a second front in Europe to ease some of the pressure on us," Stalin told the Allies.

But it was not practical at this point, the Allies replied. Churchill himself made the trip to Russia in the summer of 1942 to discuss over-all plans with Stalin. The conversations went smoothly enough until the last night when Stalin entertained him with dinner in his quarters in the Kremlin. It was an excellent meal and the atmosphere was relaxed and friendly when Churchill suddenly turned to Stalin and asked point blank about the liquidation of the peasants during collectivization.

Stalin held up both hands, his fingers extended. "Ten million," he said. "It was fearful. Four years it lasted."

Churchill was silent.

It was a simple incident but it served to remind Stalin that the West had not forgotten nor had it forgiven simply because Russia was now an ally against Hitler.

The turning point came nearly a year later, in February, 1943, with the surrender of the German Sixth Army at Stalingrad. The Russians now gained the offensive and began the slow, hard drive to push the Germans back out of Russia.

In November, the first of the historic meetings of the Allied chiefs was held at Teheran, Iran.

Stalin went to the meeting full of suspicions. "Do you know why Roosevelt and Churchill won't open a second front in Europe?" he asked Voroshilov, the general who accompanied him. "Because they want to keep us occupied in Russia. They are afraid of our influence in eastern Europe, should we push the Germans back."

His suspicions were not reflected in his manner, however, and both Franklin D. Roosevelt, President of the United States, and Winston Churchill, Prime Minister of Great Britain, found him poker-faced but agreeable, until the possibility of Russia entering the war against Japan was brought up.

Russia After World War II

"There is the matter of our neutrality pact with Japan," Stalin hedged. "Not that we do not welcome your successes against them."

"There are troops in Siberia, aren't there?" Roosevelt asked. "Couldn't they be used if you were to break the agreement?"

"In reality, we have few troops there," Stalin said hurriedly. "Just enough for defensive purposes. However, if a second front were opened, then we could move some of our troops in."

Roosevelt and Churchill exchanged glances.

"That is," Stalin went on, "as soon as Germany is defeated, we can. Right now, we are totally taken up with defending our own country against the Germans."

The agreement was made and the three of them returned to their own countries. But it was not until the following June that the Allies were able to make good their commitment by landing troops in Normandy, across the English Channel from Great Britain. By then, the Russians had managed to push the Germans out of the Ukraine and back into Poland. A short time later, Russian delegates traveled to Dumbarton Oaks, a suburb of Washington, D.C., and helped to draw up the framework for a new international organization which would be known as the United Nations.

In February, 1945, Stalin met again with Roosevelt and Churchill, this time at Yalta, a city on the Crimean peninsula which extends into the Black Sea. This time, with Germany on the defensive and the Allied armies pushing in on her from every direction, there were more concrete plans to be laid.

Stalin had been dismayed at their last conference by the others' attitude toward postwar Germany. They were too lenient in what they would demand from her, he thought. This time, he was determined to have his way. Russia would require fairly heavy reparations from Germany after the war, he told Churchill and Roosevelt. And Russians would help to occupy Germany after her defeat. Also, in return for entering the war against Japan, Russia wanted the territories returned, those she had lost to Japan in the 1904 war.

Stalin felt fairly secure in making his demands. The Allies needed him, not only against Germany, but in the war against the Japanese, too. And he was right. Before the conference ended, it had been decided to divide postwar Germany into occupation zones, with France, Great Britain, the United States and Russia each occupying specific territory. The city of Berlin, which would be inside the Russian zone, was to be similarly divided. Stalin opposed France's being given a zone; he had met Charles deGaulle, the French leader, and felt that he had an inflated opinion of himself and his country's importance, but finally agreed.

Not content with having gained these concessions from his Allies, Stalin pressed further. Why not partition Germany permanently, thus insuring that it would never again threaten any of them? Roosevelt and Churchill did not come out openly against it but they would not make any commitment. Well then, Stalin proposed, what about a seat in the General Assembly of the now-forming United Nations for each of the sixteen states that made up the Union of Soviet Socialist Republics, the U.S.S.R.? Roosevelt appeared to be embarrassed by the suggestion.

In the end, a compromise was reached. Two of the states, the Ukraine and Byelorussia, were to have memberships in addition to the U.S.S.R. membership. And Stalin would definitely enter the war against Japan within three months after Germany's defeat.

Stalin turned his attention back to more immediate problems. He had already suffered one heart attack, the year before, and it had served to make him more suspicious than ever of those around him. Was he perhaps remembering Lenin and his strokes? Several times a year, he changed the members of his personal guard. No one was too close to him to escape suspicion; his guards searched everyone who came to see him for weapons.

"You seem strange today," he said once to Nikita Khrushchev. "Why don't you look me straight in the eye? Why do you try to avoid my glance?"

As the spring progressed and the Germans retreated, Russian troops began pushing into the eastern European states on their borders. It was the opportunity the Communists had waited for. In several of the states, native Communists had managed to gain control of the police force and the army, a technique they had learned from the Russians. Now the native Communists, with the help of the Red Army, when needed, were able to gain control of the government of each state.

They were aided unwittingly by the upper classes, many of whom had been friendly to the Nazis who had conquered them. The Communists had not only been anti-Nazi but they had also supported programs of land reform, the partition of the great estates among the peasants, an idea which had great appeal to the poor and underprivileged of those nations.

As the Russian armies moved through Hungary, Rumania, Czechoslovakia and Bulgaria, they left behind them, in each case and by one means or another, a government composed of Communists whose first loyalty was to Moscow and Stalin himself. Only in Yugoslavia did they fail. There they helped install a Communist government headed by Marshal Tito, a native Yugoslavian who had distinguished himself as a leader of the partisan forces during the war, but once in command, Tito refused to follow the dictates of Moscow, preferring instead to manage his own country in his own way.

With the Russian armies pushing hard from the east, the Allies from the west and south, Germany collapsed suddenly and dramatically. On May 1, 1945, the Hamburg radio announced that Adolf Hitler was dead. On May 2, the Russians took Berlin and hostilities ended in Italy with the capture of the German commander there. On May 4, all German forces in the Netherlands, northwest Germany and Denmark surrendered to the British general, Montgomery. On May 8, the armistice was signed and the European war was officially ended.

In July, the Big Three—Russia, Great Britain, and the

United States—met again in Potsdam, Germany. But there were some changes in personnel. United States President Roosevelt had died unexpectedly in April, shortly after Stalin had given Japan the one-year notice that he wanted to terminate their neutrality pact. While the Potsdam Conference was in session, Prime Minister Churchill returned to Great Britain for the election which replaced him with Clement Attlee. By the end of the meeting, Stalin was the only one of the original three heads of state left. Harry S. Truman, Roosevelt's Vice-President and now President, was the United States representative.

Before Churchill left for London, he spoke to Stalin about the difficulties which the British ministers were having in Bulgaria. They were being treated rudely, he said, and prevented from doing their jobs. As one of the countries in which Russia had helped install a Communist government, Bulgaria was not too friendly with the Western powers.

Stalin smiled congenially. "All fairy tales," he said good-naturedly. "All fairy tales." The Western powers were not going to interfere in the countries where he had gained control. It was going to be made easier for them to withdraw than to stay there.

Stalin mentioned to Truman that he had received a second message from Japan asking him to receive a Japanese ambassador who would talk to him about the possibility of his acting as a go-between in peace talks with the Western powers. He had ignored the first message, he said, and refused the second one. Truman was silent. The United States and Great Britain had already issued an ultimatum to the Japanese people to surrender. No more could be done at the moment.

Later in the conference, he mentioned casually to Stalin that the United States had a new weapon, one of unusual destructive powers.

"I am glad to hear it," Stalin answered. "I hope you will make good use of it against Japan." He did not mention that through his spies in the United States, he was already fairly well informed on that weapon.

The Western powers were still uncertain about the secret weapon, however. It had been impossible to test it too thoroughly. They still felt that they needed Russia in the war against Japan and pressed Stalin for a definite commitment.

He first needed to make a mutual-assistance treaty with China, as he had told them at Yalta, Stalin replied. The meeting disbanded and General Chiang Kai-shek, the recognized leader of the Nationalist Chinese forces presently in exile because of the Japanese occupation, made the trip to Moscow to negotiate such a treaty. He was still there on August 6, when the first atomic bomb was exploded at Hiroshima, Japan.

The bomb destroyed more than half of the city and resulted in more than eighty thousand deaths. Even the Americans who had developed and used it seemed horrified by its tremendous power.

If the Americans were stunned, Stalin was even more so. He realized that unless he acted quickly, the war in the Pacific might end without him and the land promised him by the Allies might be lost. Two days later, on August 8, he informed the Americans that as of the next day, a state of war would exist between Russia and Japan. On August 9, Russian troops marched into Manchuria, then occupied by the Japanese, and the second atomic bomb was exploded at Nagasaki, Japan.

Less than a week later, Japan announced its willingness to surrender and World War II, after nearly six years, was finally ended.

The atomic bombs had other effects, too. The knowledge that the United States possessed such a devastating weapon seemed to reawaken Stalin's old fears of the West. From this moment on, they would find him more difficult than ever to get along with. It now became absolutely imperative to have a ring of friendly states around the borders to serve as a buffer between him and the West.

The old Communist international organization had been disbanded in 1943, as a result of the cooperation between Stalin and the Western powers. Now it was re-formed and given new life. Efforts were redoubled to win converts to communism throughout the world.

The first open challenge was made in Greece. The British had been occupying the country since the Germans had been evacuated and had been holding back a strong, militant group of Communists, supported by Moscow, who threatened to take over the government. In 1947, the British notified the Americans that they were forced to withdraw from Greece because of financial difficulties and that the Communists were ready to overthrow the government as soon as they did.

The United States, under the leadership of President Truman and Secretary of State George Marshall, answered with the Marshall Plan, a program of aid to countries threatened by such situations. Stalin's challenge had been taken up by the Americans and the "Cold War," a phrase used to describe the maneuvering for power and influence by Russia against the Western nations, began.

The second challenge came a short time later in Berlin. There had been increasing difficulties; Great Britain, France and the United States wanted to reunify the German state; Stalin did not. Stalin was using, and planned to continue using, the eastern Communist-controlled states and his zone in Germany as colonies, that is, sources for raw materials and markets for finished goods. In addition, he had carried millions of dollars' worth of equipment and machinery out of them for installation in Russia.

When the West began making economic reforms in the western zones of Germany and even restoring it to some degree of prosperity, Stalin took action. Hoping to destroy American prestige in Europe, he announced the Berlin blockade. Since Berlin was inside the Russian zone, all railroads and highways leading to it ran through that zone. To shut off the flow of American, British and French supplies to their own zones in Berlin, he closed the borders of the Russian zone to them.

It was a crucial moment. By so doing, he was deliberately running the risk of war but he gambled on the Americans and British abandoning their zones rather than entering into a "hot" war.

They did neither. Russia might control the ground access to Berlin but it did not control the skies above it. The Allies took to the air, establishing a gigantic airlift of unprecedented size. Before the Russians reopened the borders in May, 1949, the Americans and British were flying an average of eight thousand tons of food, fuel, and supplies a day.

Instead of destroying American prestige, Stalin had given it a boost. Now he was forced to cast about for other ways in which he could insure the security of Russia. One way was to bind the eastern nations more closely and this was accomplished by the Council of Economic Assistance, an alliance consisting of Russia, Poland, Bulgaria, Czechoslovakia, Hungary and Rumania. In it, the smaller nations agreed to trade with Russia and to use their factories to produce the specific kinds of machinery needed by Stalin.

Stalin was playing a similar game in the East. When the Japanese had surrendered and then withdrawn from China, Chiang Kai-shek, the Nationalist leader, had moved in to establish control. But the Chinese Communists, headed by Mao Tse-tung and Chou En-lai, were already there and were able to gain control of large areas before Chiang could reach them. Four long years of fighting ensued, but in the end, the Communists had won and Chiang had been pushed back onto the island of Formosa.

A similar vacuum had been created by the end of the war in Korea. The Allies had agreed informally that it should be independent and that it should go through a period of supervision first, but no concrete plans had been made. When the war ended suddenly and the Japanese withdrew, there was a hasty agreement between the Americans and Russians for occupation, the Russian army to be responsible for the area north of the 38th parallel, the Americans south of that line.

Two years later, the Americans had requested the United Nations to supervise elections in their zone and a democratic type of government had been set up. The Russians retaliated by setting up a Communist-controlled People's Republic in their zone. In 1949, both nations withdrew their armies of occupation.

In the United Nations, the same kind of struggle was taking place. There was no doubt in Stalin's mind that the chief aim of the United States was to destroy Communism and, in the process, the U.S.S.R. Every move the Russian delegation made, they found themselves opposed by the United States and they, in turn, opposed every move made by the United States.

The admission of Red China was an example. Russia proposed to the Security Council that the representative of Chiang Kai-shek's government on Formosa be ousted from the Council in favor of a delegate from Communist China. The United States opposed it. The Russian delegate, in a display of temperament, walked out on the meetings.

It was a costly move for the Soviet Union. When the North Koreans suddenly invaded South Korea on June 25, 1950, the United States asked for an emergency meeting of the Security Council. Without the Russian delegate present to veto the action, the Council approved a resolution declaring a breach of the peace had been committed and ordered the North Koreans to cease their actions and withdraw their forces. At a subsequent meeting, the Council called on the members of the United Nations to give assistance to South Korea. The cold war had turned hot.

But even with communism making gains around the world, Stalin was daily becoming more suspicious, more convinced that he was surrounded not only by enemies on the outside, but also by traitors in his inner circle. He trusted no one. Georgi Malenkov, who had been his personal chief Party supervisor and informer for years, was reported on by spies just as regularly as his other associates. Lavrenty Beria, Vyacheslav Molotov, Nikolai Bulganin, Lazar Kaganovich, Nikita Khrushchev—men who had been with him for years and whose personal loyalty seemed to be unquestioned—all came in for their share of suspicion. Stalin had confided to a few of his guards that he knew some of his officials were plotting to murder him.

He had more reason to doubt the satellite, or surrounding, countries. Many of them were becoming restless, discontent with the lack of rewards communism seemed to bring to their countries. In several of them, Stalin found it necessary to purge the old leaders and install new ones.

Despite the fact that Russia had now developed its own atomic bomb, his fear of the West grew. Insofar as possible, he cut off all exchange between the countries under his influence and the Western nations. There was no informational exchange, on either a scientific or a cultural level. The few visitors from the West who were allowed in found themselves restricted to certain areas, and then under the constant surveillance of the secret police. It was as though, in Winston Churchill's term, an iron curtain had descended between the Communist and the non-Communist worlds.

Even in Korea the effect was felt. The war reached a stalemate, then dragged on, the Communists refusing to discuss peace terms.

It was no surprise to anyone when in January, 1953, the Moscow newspapers carried front-page stories of a plot of Kremlin doctors to murder Stalin and several other prominent Soviet leaders. In addition, the doctors, who were variously called "monsters," "despicable misfits" and "a band of poison mixers," were charged with having already poisoned several people and having made false diagnoses and deliberately giving faulty treatments to several notable patients. It was stated that they had performed these acts as agents of the British and American secret service.

The whispers echoed through the Kremlin halls. It was the beginning of a new purge, everyone agreed. Where would it end this time? How many millions of lives would be needed to allay Stalin's suspicions and his feelings of persecution. They all trembled—and waited. Only one event could save them, the death of Stalin himself.

In the meantime, Dr. Lydia Timashuk, who had made the accusations against her colleagues, was awarded the Order of

Lenin from Stalin. The doctors' confessions were made public; they admitted two murders with more in the plotting.

Then on Sunday, March 1, Stalin, like Lenin before him, was the victim of a massive brain hemorrhage which paralyzed his right side and left him unable to speak. The news was kept secret until Wednesday when the first public acknowledgment was made over Radio Moscow.

It was a clear sunny day and the crowds gathered in the Moscow streets, awaiting further news. As the day progressed and no news came, clouds formed slowly, shutting out the sun and dispensing little flurries of snow. The masses of people stood silently, waiting.

It was Thursday before the next bulletin was issued. "During Wednesday night and the first half of today, Joseph Stalin's condition became worse. At eight this morning, there developed signs of a collapse. He never regained consciousness. He died at 9:50 A.M."

The radio pleaded with the people to be orderly and calm. The wintry wind howled around the towers of the Kremlin. Joseph Stalin, the self-styled dictator of the Union of Soviet Socialist Republics, was dead.

There were other reminders of Lenin, too: the lying in state at the House of Trade Unions, the honor guard made up of top officials, the thousands who streamed by the coffin. Then on Monday morning, March 9, the body was brought to Red Square for the funeral. Immediately behind the glass-domed coffin in the funeral procession marched Georgi Malenkov. Did this mean he was to be Stalin's successor? they all wondered.

After hours of oratory, Stalin was placed beside Lenin in the special mausoleum which had been built for Lenin. Seven minutes after the doors closed, the mourning period was officially ended. Look ahead, not back, Radio Moscow urged the people.

But what was there to look ahead to? What was to happen now?

★ FOURTEEN

It was June, 1953. Joseph Stalin had been dead a little more than three months and on the surface, at least, very little had changed. Georgi Malenkov had taken over Stalin's old positions as Secretary of the Party and as Premier, or Chairman of the Council of Ministers, but that had been expected.

His resignation from the post of Party Secretary two short weeks later had caused some surprise but the job had been passed quietly to Nikita Khrushchev, another long-time supporter of Stalin's, and the impression remained that nothing had changed. Even the anti-Russian riots in the satellite states of East Germany and Czechoslovakia served to deepen the impression; they were put down quickly and brutally, just as Joseph Stalin would have done.

There had been one sour note: shortly after Stalin's death, Lavrenty Beria had been reappointed chief of the MVD, the combined Department of the Interior and the secret police. Almost immediately Beria had announced that the "doctors' plot," dreamed up by Stalin as an excuse to start a new purge, was a mistake. The surviving doctors were released, along with other political prisoners, and the Order of Lenin was taken away from Dr. Timashuk.

These were the only bits of evidence in the tremendous struggle for power that was presently taking place within the walls of the Kremlin, a struggle that was to enter a new phase this night of June 26, 1953.

An emergency meeting of the Presidium, the new name for the old Politburo, had been called. Each member was searched for weapons as he entered, then allowed to proceed

to the conference room. Each avoided the others' eyes, talking only in monosyllables. In the next room were several
Army officers armed with machine guns.

"Why are they here?" Lavrenty Beria asked.

"We are going to review defense problems," someone answered.

Beria shrugged and took his seat.

At last, they were all assembled, the fat Malenkov, sober-
faced Molotov, Khrushchev, unusually silent, the sharp-
eyed and suspicious Beria, and all the others. Then the doors
were closed.

As though a signal had been given, the others turned to
Beria. "Is it true you have been preparing to overthrow
the government?"

"Are you getting support from the British and the Americans?"

"Have you been playing a double game, seeming to be with
us while you are actually against us?"

On and on the questions went. No, Beria insisted. No, no,
no! As the time passed, the questions became more insistent,
the answers more fearful. "No, comrades, no!"

Four hours, four long hours of questions with only one
answer, "No."

But the others were not convinced. They retired to the
next room to talk it over. Was he guilty? Had he been plotting against them? They had never really trusted him; he
was too secretive, too ambitious. He was a threat to each
of them. They had been following him for weeks, they knew
everyone he had seen, every place he had gone. They were
sure he was plotting to seize power for himself, shutting them
out.

Most important of all, he did have control over a large
army of secret police and several divisions of special troops
as well as huge stores of military supplies. It had been a
mistake to let one man achieve that much power. If he
tried a coup against them, he might well succeed.

They returned to the room, their verdict decided. He was
guilty, they were sure of that, but they did not have legal

evidence. They were sure, too, that it would not be safe to allow him to go free to continue his plotting. Behind them trailed the Army officers, machine guns ready.

As Beria jumped to his feet, the machine guns coughed briefly and decisively. Lavrenty Beria lay dead on the floor. He would plot no more against the members of the Presidium.

To insure against another such threat, the MVD was broken up into several agencies which would be responsible to top members of the government.

The surface was again calm, but underneath, the struggle continued. Malenkov, realizing the shakiness of his position, cast about him for ways in which he might win the support of the people. Import more food and manufacture more consumer goods, he decided. Make the people comfortable and happy and they will keep you in power. They have suffered long enough. He gave the orders to ease restrictions.

"He is ruining the Russian economy," his enemies whispered behind his back.

"He is sacrificing our defense for luxuries," they told each other.

Nikita Khrushchev, now First Secretary of the Party, could afford to smile slyly. He was well aware that Joseph Stalin had attained his power from this same beginning and he knew, too, how it had been done. Working quietly, Khrushchev began his campaign as Stalin had begun his: by seeing to it that his own men were appointed to the positions of power in the provincial parties.

Even inside Russia, few people knew much about Nikita Khrushchev. He had been born in 1894 in the village of Kalinovka, three hundred miles south of Moscow. His father was a poor peasant, one of the many in that area who farmed in the summer, then went south in the winter to work in the mines in an effort to keep his family fed. The boy Nikita joined him in the mines at the early age of fifteen, leaving school to do so.

But the impoverished life of the peasant had little appeal for the ambitious Nikita. He worked himself up to a mechanic's job in the mines, where he stayed throughout the first World War. During these years, he took on extra responsibilities, first a wife, then in 1916, a daughter, and two years later, a son. It was around the time of his son's birth that he joined the Communist Party, and despite his family obligations, immediately joined the Red Army, too.

After four years of civil war, he returned to the mines and his family. Twenty-eight years old now, Khrushchev wanted something more than a life of hardship in the mines. He was elected Secretary of the Communist Party unit there, but this was not enough. To get ahead, one needed an education. He enrolled in the Workers' University, graduating three years later. During the years of struggle, his wife died and in 1924, while still at the University, he married again, a plump, good-natured young woman named Nina Petrovna. Three daughters and two sons were born to them.

It was after his graduation that he received his first political appointment: Party Secretary of a tiny district. Four years later, he moved to Moscow and a more important post. But Moscow had something else to offer—the chance to enroll in the famed Industrial Academy, an institution for training young Communist leaders.

From that point, he had risen rapidly in the Party. Beginning as Party chief of one of Moscow's boroughs, he moved to the Moscow City Party Committee, then to a position on the Central Committee of the Party. Through his devotion and his ability to carry through any job assigned to him, he was soon noticed by Stalin himself and given more and more important tasks. During World War II, he served his country well in directing some of the guerrilla warfare which harassed the Nazis.

At the end of the war, he was a lieutenant general with a chest full of medals—a long way from the peasant boy who had quit school at fifteen. There were Party positions waiting for him and when Stalin died, he was made a member of the Presidium, the policy-making body of the Party, and one of the five members of the Secretariat, the Party's executive body. And from those positions, he could begin his undercover campaign for power.

There was some evidence that his campaign was beginning to be successful. More and more frequently, Khrushchev appeared in public along with Malenkov, or sometimes, instead of Malenkov. Nikolai Bulganin, a World War II Red Army general and now Minister of War and Deputy Premier, began taking a bigger share of the spotlight, too.

The biggest change appeared to be in Russia's attitude toward the rest of the world. A peace treaty was finally arranged with the Communists in Korea; friendly overtures were made to China and Yugoslavia. During the Stalinist era, there had been very little communication with the Western World; now travel was made easier for visitors, a treaty was signed with the United States providing for exchange appearances of musical groups, television programs, sports teams, and artists. The rigid controls on Russian writers, artists, poets and musicians were relaxed a little.

An even bigger change was brewing. In February, 1955, at the meeting of the Supreme Soviet, Russia's legislature, the speaker raised his hand for silence and began reading from a paper in front of him. Premier Georgi Malenkov sat at one side of the hall, his head bowed. The delegates listened in stunned silence.

"I ask that I be relieved of my post as Premier and that another comrade with more experience in the field of government work be placed in my position. I recognize clearly that my insufficient experience has had negative consequences. [Signed] Georgi Malenkov."

The speaker had scarcely finished reading the paper, the audience still sat in quiet astonishment, when Nikita Khrushchev jumped to his feet.

"In the name of the Central Committee of the Communist Party of the Soviet Union," he said, "I nominate the true son of the Communist Party, the worthy pupil of the

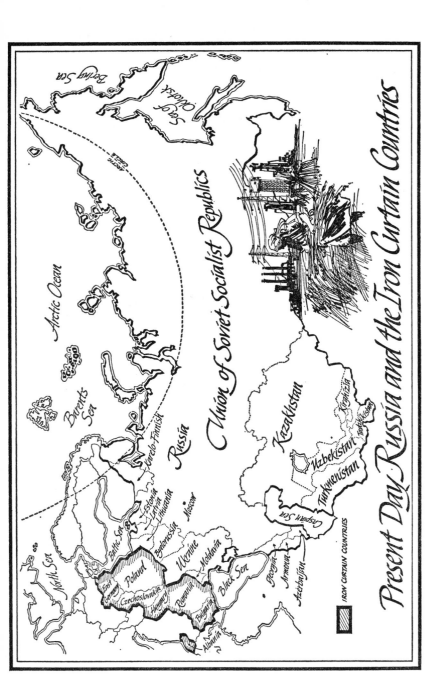

Present Day Russia and the Iron Curtain Countries

great Lenin, the close colleague of Lenin's successor, Joseph Stalin, the First Deputy Premier, Nikolai Bulganin, to be the new Soviet Premier."

The startled delegates elected Bulganin by acclamation. Georgi Malenkov was made Minister for Power Stations, a far cry from his former importance, and his program of consumer goods manufacture was promptly abandoned in favor of further strengthening heavy industry and weapons.

It was a year before the next upheaval occurred. The occasion was the Twentieth Congress of the Communist Party in Moscow. Its 1436 delegates had been meeting for eleven days; now they were called back to a special meeting at midnight, a secret meeting that they were to discuss with no one. Nikita Khrushchev mounted the speaker's platform. He began by talking about the "cult of personality," a term used to mean deifying a person and giving all one's loyalty to him instead of to the Party. He went on to say that Joseph Stalin had built such a cult of worshippers.

"The objective of the present report is not a thorough evaluation of Stalin's life and activity," he said. "At present we are concerned with a question which has immense importance to the Party now and for the future—with how the cult of the person of Stalin has been gradually growing."

He went on to read, publicly, for the first time, Lenin's Testament and a letter written by Krupskaya to Trotsky about Lenin's distrust of Stalin. Many of the young Communists, growing up during the Stalinist era, had not heard of the documents and there was a rustle of noise from the audience, a surprised intake of breath. They had been taught all their lives, in everything they read, saw or heard, that Stalin was all-good and all-wise. Now Nikita Khrushchev was summoning up the ghosts of the dead leaders to prove that he was not. The whole struggle with Zinoviev and Kamenev, the murder of Kerov, the notorious purge trials, every crime of Stalin's was laid bare to the delegates.

Now and then, as the report continued, tracing Stalin's career from its beginnings, there was an undercurrent of stirring in the hall, whispers, foot-shuffling, uneasiness. It was nearing daylight when the report finally ended. It was only along toward the end that the delegates found their voices again. There were a few comments called out from the floor, smatterings of applause, then finally, a tension-breaking wave of laughter and tumultuous applause, the delegates rising to their feet and cheering the now-smiling Khrushchev.

It was a moment of triumph for the roly-poly Khrushchev. No longer would Russia have to be ruled in the name of a ghost; Stalin was finally buried.

The extent of the de-Stalinization became more obvious as time went on. At the Party Congress, Khrushchev had stated that peaceful coexistence with the West was a possibility; this was a new note, a new idea to come from Communist Russia. In effect, he was denying one of the bases of the beliefs held by both Lenin and Stalin: that war between the communist and capitalist countries was inevitable. Khrushchev was saying that peace between the U.S.S.R. and the rest of the world was a possibility, that they could both exist on this planet, each pursuing its own goals and its own way of life without the necessity of war. As a first step in carrying out this new change in attitude, Stalin's old supporter Vyacheslav Molotov was dismissed as Foreign Minister.

There were to be serious consequences. In the satellite countries, Molotov's name had been synonymous with a tough foreign policy and with keeping the satellites strictly in the Communist orbit. His dismissal was thought to mean a relaxation in both areas. The first testing of the policy came within a month.

The trouble started with a few workers in the highly industrialized city of Poznan, Poland, one of the satellite countries. Their immediate concern was a demand for better wages and greater rights but their discontent went far deeper than that, as the Russian Communists knew full well. A few strikes were called, then suddenly the affair became a major rebellion, with thousands of workers roaming the streets, shouting "Bread and freedom!" and clashing bloodily with the security police.

Khrushchev hurried to Warsaw, the capital of Poland. It was obvious that some concessions must be made or the Russians would have to use considerable military force to keep the Polish Communists in power in that country. Khrushchev compromised; Vladislav Gomulka, a popular but independent Communist who had been jailed years before by Stalin, was released and allowed to take office. Khrushchev felt, with good reason, that Gomulka could be controlled by the Russians once he was in office.

The Hungarians, seeing the Polish success, decided to take matters into their own hands. The all-Communist government was ousted and a coalition government which included several anti-Communists was installed. From behind barricades made of furniture, with home-made weapons or simply with clubs, Hungarian students and workers fought for their rights against the political police. In Budapest, the capital, local Communists were savagely massacred and hung head down from the trees that lined the streets.

Over and over, the Hungarian rebel radio called to the west: "S.O.S. Send medicines. Send arms. S.O.S."

Then there was silence. The Red Army had arrived in force. More than twenty thousand men, women, and children were slaughtered in the course of a few days; a new puppet ruler was installed; the rebellion was over.

It was obvious that the Russian leaders had made a mistake with the de-Stalinization campaign. Anti-Stalinism had somehow been translated into anti-Communism. They began to backtrack a little. Stalin had not been all bad, they said swiftly.

At a New Year's party, Khrushchev tried to make their position clearer. "When it comes to the struggle against imperialism," he said, "we are all good Stalinists."

So far as the Western World was concerned, Stalinism and de-Stalinization did not seem very far apart. At the United Nations, the West had become accustomed to the sound of "nyet!" (the Russian word for "no") under Stalin and his successors. In the matter of reunifying Germany, an effective end to the arms race, and all other controversial matters,

Russia seemed to be following about the same course as ever. In response to the North Atlantic Treaty Organization, the mutual defense pact signed by the Western nations, Russia had fostered a Warsaw Pact, a similar agreement which included the U.S.S.R. and its satellites.

But the Warsaw Pact did not solve Russia's difficulties. There was another riot in Poland to be put down; the rift with China was growing daily, despite Russian attempts to solve it; the internal struggle for power was still going on.

The struggle for power in the outside world was still going on, too, but Khrushchev had given it a new twist. Khrushchev appeared just as determined as Stalin to win the world for communism, but his tactics were totally different. There were few countries he did not visit, and in most of them, he won a quick reputation for friendliness and good-nature.

In Czechoslovakia, Khrushchev told the crowd who came to welcome him, "The Soviet voice will always be the voice of peace."

In Denmark, he visited a war memorial, a kindergarten class, and a shipyard, talking peace and disarmament with each listener.

In Yugoslavia, he insisted to reporters that the "relationship between Yugoslavia and the U.S.S.R. is eternal."

"Let us talk about the question of how best to improve relations between us and the United States," he said to a visiting American.

But he remembered always the basic conflict between the Russian and American ways of life. "When the last spadeful of earth is thrown on the grave of capitalism," he told the Chinese ambassador in Moscow, "we will do it together with China."

And again in Yugoslavia: "What is the most important problem now? It is to beat capitalism. The one who creates the most through mass production will win."

Khrushchev was away on another of these "good-will" trips when a special meeting of the Presidium was called early in July, 1957. The business at hand: to dismiss Khrushchev from his position as Party Secretary. Malenkov and Molotov, both of whom had been demoted but left to continue as members of the Presidium, led the opposition. When the vote was taken, they had won. Khrushchev was out.

But it was not to end so simply. Khrushchev, knowing that he had a majority in the Central Committee, if not in the Presidium, demanded that the decision be referred to them. The Presidium could not refuse; to do so would turn the Central Committee against them. The Central Committee not only vetoed their action, it ended by ousting Malenkov and Molotov.

But there was one difference to be noted: instead of executing them as had been done with political outcasts in the past, they were given minor posts and sent to Siberia, still alive and healthy.

Premier Bulganin had chosen the wrong side. In the Presidium voting, he had sided with Malenkov and Molotov. When Khrushchev refused to accept the decision, Bulganin protested. "But we are seven and you are four," he said, referring to the vote.

"In mathematics, two and two are indeed four," Khrushchev replied, "but that does not apply to politics. There things are different."

How different, Bulganin was to discover shortly. In March of the following year, he presented his resignation to the newly elected Supreme Soviet, the national legislature, as custom demanded. To his surprise, however, the resignation was accepted. One of the delegates rose quickly to his feet.

"Upon instruction of the Central Committee of the Communist Party of the Soviet Union," he said, "I propose to name Comrade Nikita Khrushchev Chairman of the Council of Ministers and to charge him with forming a cabinet and submitting it to the Supreme Soviet."

He added that Khrushchev should retain his position as First Secretary of the Communist Party, the same kind of dual arrangement Stalin had had. His proposal was adopted by acclamation.

"I will serve my people and my Party faithfully," Khrushchev said in accepting the office, "and I will spare neither strength nor health nor life itself . . . to build a Communist society in our land."

Nor did he spare himself in attempting to bring a Communist society to other countries. He and other ministers in the Presidium redoubled their efforts to create friendly feelings toward Russia on the part of other nations throughout the world. Controls on the satellite countries were relaxed slightly. Anastas Mikoyan, a swarthy, energetic, longtime member of the Presidium, visited the United States in a kind of good-will tour. Frol Kozlov, Khrushchev's friend and supporter, personally opened the Soviet Exhibition of Science and Technology in New York, visited with United States President Dwight D. Eisenhower and made a whirlwind tour of the country.

In return, Vice-President Richard Nixon journeyed to Moscow to open the American National Exposition, another part of the cultural exchange program. His reception was an example of the peculiar relations between the two nations. Everywhere he went, he was toasted and entertained but there was another side to the visit, a side which betrayed the basic hostility between the two most powerful countries the world had ever seen.

During a visit to the Exposition, Nixon made a remark which Khrushchev did not understand about major powers "dictating" to other nations.

"Don't try to threaten us," Khrushchev answered angrily. "We will answer your threats with threats. We have means at our disposal which can have very bad consequences for you."

Nixon poked him in the chest with his finger. "So have we," he said bluntly.

Khrushchev smiled grimly. "But ours are better," he said.

On the whole, however, the visit was highly successful and resulted in Khrushchev himself visiting the United States a few months later. His wife, Nina, accompanied him and they visited farms and cities across the United States, complimenting the Americans on their skills in some respects, particularly in making hot dogs, which Khrushchev called "their superiority in sausage-making."

He also took advantage of the opportunity to urge a meeting "at the summit," a top-level conference of Western and Russian officials in an attempt to iron out some of the differences between the two. President Eisenhower agreed to meet with him in Paris the following year, 1960. However, Eisenhower added, he could stay only seven days. Should the conference last longer, Vice-President Nixon would have to take his place.

"That would be like leaving the cabbage to the care of the goat," Khrushchev snorted. Nixon's visit to Russia had not endeared him to Khrushchev.

The prospect of the conference did not halt Khrushchev's attempts to win allies for the U.S.S.R., however. In February, 1960, he signed a trade agreement with Fidel Castro, the Cuban dictator who had come to power in that country as a result of the military overthrow of the previous government, a corrupt regime that had had little support from the Cuban people.

Help was also given to Egypt in the construction of a large dam after American aid had been offered, then withdrawn. The Egyptian dictator, Gamal Abdel Nasser, became noticeably more friendly to Russia.

Khrushchev stepped up his visits abroad, hoping to be able to bring enough pressure to bear on the Western World through his contacts with neutral nations so that the West would be forced to agree to some of his proposals.

As the time for the conference grew nearer, it was obvious that his tactics were not going to work. The Summit Conference would end in the same stalemate as past conferences. In order to claim a diplomatic victory, he needed an excuse for breaking up the conference before it began. Unwittingly, the Americans gave it to him.

Shortly before the conference, an American U-2 plane was shot down over central Russia and its pilot captured along with much high-powered camera equipment.

The Americans have been spying on us, Khrushchev charged triumphantly.

The American reply was frank enough to take the Russians completely off guard. "It is certainly no secret that, given the state of the world today, intelligence collection activities are practiced by all countries." Particularly since Russia has been so secretive, the American State Department announced, planes have been making flights along Soviet borders for four years.

It was all the excuse Khrushchev needed. The conference ended before it began with his refusal to deal with the Americans since they had admitted spying on his country.

Two other events occurring that month were completely overshadowed by the outburst in Paris by Khrushchev. In Moscow, Alexander Kosygin, the former Minister of Light Industry, moved up a notch to become First Deputy Premier and Leonid Brezhnev became President of the Supreme Soviet. Kosygin, a native of Leningrad, had once been a favorite of Stalin's, then had fallen from grace. He had held many different Party posts and was thought to be a firm supporter of Khrushchev's "coexistence" policy. Brezhnev was also known as a protégé of Khrushchev's, a hardworking Party official who had risen gradually.

And in Mexico City, the almost forgotten Jaime Ramón Hernández del Rio Mercader was released from prison, having served his twenty-year term for the murder of Leon Trotsky. Two Czechoslovakian diplomats hurried him to the airport where he departed for Cuba and disappeared without a trace.

Natalia Trotsky noted the event. "He is going to his reward—or his elimination," she told reporters. Neither she nor the rest of the world was to know which it was.

The failure of the Paris Conference did not change Khrushchev's position, however. In November, at an international gathering of Communists from eighty-seven nations, Khrushchev spoke about the need for peaceful coexistence.

"A nuclear war would destroy civilization," he told the delegates, "and must be avoided." Contrary to the former

Communist position, "armed revolution must not be resorted to recklessly, lest it precipitate world war," he went on. "There must be negotiation of differences between the communist and capitalist worlds, not simply to avoid war but because as time passes, communism will grow strong while capitalism grows weak."

Not all the assembled delegates agreed with him. The men from China, Albania and North Vietnam felt that he was deserting basic communist philosophy.

Was Khrushchev serious or was he merely trying to lull the West into a false sense of security? many people wondered. A part of the answer came in October, 1962. United States reconnaissance planes flying over Cuba took photographs which showed beyond doubt that the Russian "trade agreement" had become something else entirely. Russian missiles capable of hurling fifty times the destructive power of the Hiroshima bomb were poised on Cuban soil and aimed at the United States and Latin American countries.

United States President John F. Kennedy who had succeeded Eisenhower in January, 1961, acted promptly. On nationwide television, he told the nation: "We have two goals, to prevent the use of these missiles against this or any other country and to secure their withdrawal or elimination from the Western Hemisphere."

Russia must dismantle and take away the missiles immediately, Kennedy said. If not, the United States would remove them by invasion. An aggressive act from Cuba would be treated as an attack by the Soviet Union itself, he went on, and the United States would retaliate against Russia with the sudden and full force of its thermonuclear might.

The reaction was instantaneous and world-wide. People braced themselves for war. American ships formed a blockade around the island of Cuba, just ninety miles off their southern shore.

Khrushchev sputtered and blustered—but, less than two weeks later, he agreed to the withdrawal of the missiles. To save face with the other nations of the world, he claimed credit for preserving peace by his move. He called for a continued "exchange of opinions on the prohibition of atomic and thermonuclear weapons and on general disarmament," at the same time.

President Kennedy answered him in kind. "It is my earnest hope," he said, "that the governments of the world can . . . turn their earnest attention to the compelling necessity for ending the arms race and reducing world tension."

"Who won and who lost?" Khrushchev said later to reporters. "Reason won."

Alexander Kosygin, First Deputy Premier, saluted the "concessions by both sides to peace and sanity."

Both sides found themselves able to make even greater concessions less than a year later at a conference in Moscow. After weeks of preparation, in 1963 ministers from both countries and Great Britain signed a limited test-ban treaty, outlawing nuclear weapons testing in the atmosphere, outer space, or under water. Other nations of the world were invited to participate in the treaty.

The response came from all over the world. From some, like Japan, it was unqualified approval. From others, like Communist China, it was bitter criticism. "Khrushchev has committed an act of betrayal," Chinese leaders charged.

The widening rift with China caused serious consternation among some Russian officials even though Nikita Khrushchev seemed unconcerned about it. It was one of the reasons for the secret meeting of the Party's Central Committee in October, 1964, while Khrushchev was vacationing on the Black Sea. One of the members of the Presidium was sent to bring Khrushchev back with him.

Suspecting that something was wrong, Khrushchev made hurried excuses to some visitors and rushed back to Moscow by plane. At the airport, a long black limousine stood waiting to drive him to the meeting.

Before he had an opportunity to ask what the meeting was about, he found himself under attack. It was four hours before he had a chance to answer the charges that he was "trying to start a new cult of personality," that he was "unable to control himself," that he "made long, boring speeches" and that he had adopted a "provocative attitude" toward Red China. More seriously, they charged that his economic policies, particularly his agricultural policy, were failures.

Khrushchev's answer was as long as the attack had been. Furiously angry, he defended himself against the charges, showering curses and invectives on his attackers.

"You see, Comrades," one of them said when he had finally finished, "it is impossible to talk to him."

As he had done before when the Presidium had attempted to oust him, Khrushchev demanded that the matter be referred to the Central Committee. This time, however, they were ready for him.

"The members of the Central Committee are assembled and waiting," one of the Presidium ministers told him.

In the general meeting hall, Khrushchev tried to speak to the delegates but they shouted him down. A vote was taken. His opponents had a bare majority. Khrushchev was out.

Not one, but two, men took over his positions. Alexander Kosygin, First Deputy Premier, now became Premier, or Chairman of the Council of Ministers. Leonid Brezhnev, President of the Supreme Soviet, was promoted to First Secretary of the Party.

What kind of men were these? How long would they last? No one could answer either question. The new leaders hastened to assure the world that there would be no basic changes in policy. Except, they added hurriedly, "Moscow will take the initiative in trying to overcome difficulties within the Communist movement," a direct promise to try to heal the split between the U.S.S.R. and Communist China. At a speech in Red Square, in front of the Kremlin, Brezhnev promised "continued emphasis on production of consumer goods," Kosygin, "greater investment in heavy industry."

What did the Russians think of their new leaders? They appeared to be too accustomed to sudden changes in leadership to be very concerned.

"I guess he's—what's his name?—he's all right," one citizen said.

After their first year in office, reaction to Brezhnev and Kosygin was still lukewarm.

"They're going to have to do something big before the people feel that they know anything more about them than their names," another citizen said.

What had they done? It was largely a matter of opinion and many people felt they had done little. Mostly, they had continued Khrushchev's basic policies but without his flair for dramatizing his actions. They had made a few changes, but with uncertainty and seeming confusion. One of the changes came in agriculture, an area where Khrushchev had failed flagrantly. When the 1965 crops were harvested, it appeared that Brezhnev and Kosygin had done no better. It was still necessary to purchase wheat from abroad to feed Russia's millions. In industry, the reports were similar—the slight changes made had brought little or no results.

In international relations, Russia's new image was quite different from the handshaking, flamboyant Khrushchev. The Kremlin was quieter than it had been since the days of the tsars.

"Everyone is a lot calmer now," one Russian summed it up.

Even Nikita Khrushchev himself seemed much calmer. In one of his rare public appearances several months after his removal from office, reporters and friends clustered about him.

"How do you feel?" they called to him.

"I feel like a pensioner," he answered quietly. "All right."

But the fact that he and his wife, Nina, were still alive and in Moscow rather than the victims of secret execution or exile appeared to many people as the most significant change of all. Was it possible that the Russian nation was becoming more like the democracies of the West? Throughout the world, people noted the changes: the peaceful transfer of power, the use of the profit motive in agriculture and industry, production based on consumers' demands, the less frequent and less violent verbal attacks on the United States and other Western nations. Were they signs of real and permanent change? Or were they simply another phase in the vast, colorful panorama of revolutionary Russia?

Only history could provide the final answer.

Other Interesting Reading on Russia

Course of Russian History, The, by Melvin Wren. Macmillan Company, New York, 1963.

History of Russia, A, by Jesse D. Clarkson. Random House, New York, 1961.

History of the Russian Revolution, The, by Leon Trotsky. Simon and Schuster, New York, 1932.

Karl Marx, by Isaiah Berlin. Oxford University Press, New York, 1963.

Khrushchev and Stalin's Ghost, by Bertram D. Wolfe. Frederick Praeger, New York, 1957.

Life and Death of Lenin, The, by Robert Payne. Simon and Schuster, New York, 1964.

Life of Lenin, The, by Louis Fischer. Harper and Row, New York, 1964.

Mind of an Assassin, The, by Isaac Don Levine. Farrar, Strauss, and Cudahy, New York, 1959.

Romanovs, The, by William Gerhardi. G. P. Putnam's Sons, New York, 1939.

Russia Revisited, by Louis Fischer. Doubleday Company, New York, 1957.

Secret History of Stalin's Crimes, The, by Alexander Orlov. Random House, 1953.

Ten Days That Shook the World, by John Reed. Random House, New York, 1960.

Three Who Made a Revolution, by Bertram D. Wolfe. Dell Publishing, New York, 1964.

To the Finland Station, by Edmund Wilson. Doubleday Company, New York, 1940.

Index

Agelhoff, Sylvia, 11, 16
Albania, 182
Allies, World War I, 80, 96, 108, 109, 115, 150. World War II, 154, 156, 158-160, 164
Alma Ata, 139, 140
America. *See* United States of America
American National Exposition, 179
Archangel, 109
Assembly of Russian Factory and Mill Workers, 50
Attlee, Clement, 161
atom bomb, 161, 162, 166
Aurora, 88, 90-92
Austria/Austrians, 108
Austria-Hungary, 68
Axis powers, World War II. *See* by individual names

Babeuf, Gracchus, 24, 25, 38
Bakunin, Michael, 38
Balkan Mountains, 68
Baltic Sea, 22, 54
Baltic states. *See* by individual names
Batu, 19
Batum, 67
Belgium/Belgians, 15, 48
Beria, Lavrenty, 148, 165, 168-170
Berlin airlift, 164
Berlin blockade, 163
Black Hundreds, 58
Black Sea, 54, 158, 183
blitzkreig (of Great Britain), 10
Bloody Sunday, 50-53, 57, 61, 62
Blue House, 146, 147
Bolsheviks/Bolshevism, 49, 54, 62, 63, 66-68, 78, 80-90, 93-95, 97, 99, 100, 102-108, 132, 136-138, 144, 148, 150
Brest-Litovsk, treaty of. *See* Treaties
Brezhnev, Leonid, 181, 184, 185
Bronstein, Lev. *See* Trotsky, Leon
Bulganin, Nikolai, 165, 172, 174, 178
Bulgaria, 160, 161, 164
Byelorussia, 151, 159

Cadets. *See* Constitutional Democrats

cadets, military, 89, 91, 93, 97, 99
calendar, Gregorian, 108. Russian, 21
Castro, Fidel, 180
Central Committee, 68, 127, 128, 130, 135-137, 171, 172, 178, 184
Cheka, 110, 114, 117, 124, 127, 134, 138
Chelyabinsk, 109
Chiang Kai-shek, 162, 164, 165
China/Chinese, 18, 162, 164, 165, 172, 177, 182-184
Chou En-lai, 164
Christianity/Christians, 24, 69
Churchill, Winston, 154, 156, 158, 159, 161, 166
class struggle, doctrine of, 32
co-existence, 175, 181
Cold War, 163
collectivization, 141-143, 156
Commission on Political Terrorism, 147
Committee of Salvation, 94, 97
Committee to Fight Counterrevolution, 84
Communist International, 136, 150, 162
Communist League, 28
Communist Manifesto, 28, 30, 32
Congress of the Russian Social Democratic Labor Party (Russian Communist Party), First, 44, Second, 48, Eleventh, 119, Thirteenth, 126, Fourteenth, 134, Tenth Anniversary of the Revolution (1927), 137, 138, Twentieth, 174, 175
Conspiracy of Equals, 24
Constituent Assembly, 102-106
Constitution of Power, decree on, 97
Constitutional Democrats, 57, 76
Cossacks, 34, 35, 51, 52, 97, 99, 110
Council of Economic Assistance, 164
Council of Ministers, 168, 178, 184
Council of Peoples' Commissars, 97, 119, 128
Council of the Republic, 90
Cuba, 180-182

187

Czechoslovakia/Czechoslovakians, 108, 109, 147, 160, 164, 168, 177, 181

Dead Sea, 24
Decembrist Revolt, 27
DeGaulle, Charles, 159
Denmark/Danes, 160, 177
de-Stalinization, 175, 176
Dewey, John, 147
Djugashvili, Ekaterina, 67
Djugashvili, Joseph (Soso). *See* Stalin, Joseph
doctors' plot, 166, 167
Duma, national, 53-55, 57, 61-63, 65, 69, 71-74, 76
Dumas, city, 33, 56, 94
Dumbarton Oaks, 158

Egypt, 180
Eisenhower, Dwight, 179, 180, 182
Ekaterinburg, 111, 112
Emancipation of Labor, League for, 38, 40
Engels, Freidrich, 28-32
England/English, 10, 109, 115, 147, 150, 152, 154, 156, 158-161, 163, 164, 166, 169, 183. London, 28, 54, 66, 161. Manchester, 31
English Channel, 158
Essenes, 24
Estonia, 107, 151

Fedor, 20
Fighting Union for Liberation of the Working Class, 43
Finland/Finns, 62, 84, 151. Vyborg, 65, 88, 95, 151. War with, 151
Finland Station, 78
First International Workingmen's Association, 38
Five Year Plans, 143, 146, 148, 149
Formosa, 164
Fourth International, 15, 148, 151
France/French, 23, 25, 30, 80, 108, 109, 115, 147, 150, 159, 163. Paris, 100, 147, 180, 181
Franz Joseph, 68
French Revolution, 23, 24, 55

Gachina, 99
Gapon, Father George, 50-52, 54, 62
Genghis Khan, 18, 19
Georgia, 66, 107, 115, 122, 123
Germany/Germans, 10, 21, 25, 28-30, 41, 44, 70, 71, 77, 80-85, 107, 108, 118, 137, 146, 149, 150, 152, 153, 155, 156, 158-160, 163, 168, 176. Berlin, 150, 159, 160, 163. Hamburg, 160. Potsdam, 161
Gomulka, Vladislav, 176
Gorki, 119, 122, 124, 126, 127
G.P.U., 15
Great Britain. *See* England
Great Terror, 143, 149
Greece/Greeks, 20, 24, 163

Hansen, Joseph, 11-15
Harte (guard), 9, 10
Hawaii. *See* Pearl Harbor
Hebrews, 24
history, interpretations of, 31, 32
Hitler, Adolf, 10, 146, 149, 151, 152, 154-156, 160
House of Trade Unions, 127, 167
Hungary/Hungarians, 109, 160, 164, 176
Igor, 17
Industrial Revolution, 25, 31
Iran, 156
Iskra (The Spark), 44, 45, 47, 49
Italy/Italians, 20, 153
Ivan I (Kalita), 19
Ivan III (The Great), 19, 20
Ivan IV (The Terrible), 20
Izvestia, 56

Jacson, Frank, 11-14, 16, 151, 156, 158
Japan, 49, 54, 56, 150, 153, 154, 158, 159, 161, 162, 164, 183. Hiroshima, 162, 182. Nagasaki, 162
Joffe, Adolph, 137, 138
Joffe, Mrs. Adolph, 139, 140
Joint Commission of Inquiry, 147

Kaganovich, Lazar, 165
Kalinovka, 170
Kamenev, Leo, 66, 68, 77, 85, 91, 95, 97, 120, 124, 131, 132, 134-139, 143-146, 174

Kaplan, Fanny, 113, 114
Kazan, 40. Cathedral, 52
Kennedy, John F., 182, 183
Kerensky, Alexander, 73, 76, 79, 81-90, 91, 93, 99, 100
Kerov, 143, 144, 174
Khrushchev, Nikita, 150, 159, 165, 168-172, 174-185
Khrushchev, Nina, 171, 179, 185
Kiev, 17
Korea, 164-166, 172
Korean War, 165, 166, 172
Kornilov, Lavr, 83-85
Kosygin, Alexander, 181, 183-185
Kozlov, Frol, 179
Krasnov, Peter, 99
Kremlin, 97, 108, 114, 117, 121, 122, 128, 135, 146, 153, 156, 166-168, 184, 185
Kremlin Clinic, 133
Kremlin Palace, Great, 121
Krupskaya, Nadezhda, 42-46, 49, 53, 68, 69, 95, 104, 117-126, 128-131, 174

Labor Party, 73
Lake Ilmen, 17
Land and Freedom, 34, 36, 38
Last Testament (Lenin's), 122, 123, 130, 131, 174
Latvia, 107, 151
League for the Emancipation of Labor. See Emancipation of Labor, League for
League of Nations, 147
League of the Just, 28
Lena River, 44
Lend-Lease Program, 154
Lenin, N. (Vladimir), 39, 40, 42-45, 48, 49, 53, 54, 59, 60, 62, 63, 67-69, 73, 77-86, 88-91, 95-97, 101, 104-106, 108, 110, 111, 113, 114, 116-128, 130, 131, 133, 137, 143, 148, 150, 155, 159, 167, 174, 175
Leningrad, 129, 137, 153-155, 181
Lithuania, 107, 151
Lvov, Prince George, 76, 80, 83

Malenkov, Georgi, 165, 167-170, 172, 174, 178

Manchuria, 162
Mao Tse-tung, 164
March Revolution, 73, 74
Marshall, George, 163
Marshall Plan, 163
Martov, Julius, 42-44, 48, 49, 66
Marx, Karl, 28-32, 34, 38, 40, 66, 119
Marxism, 38, 40, 42, 46, 47, 66
Maryinsky Palace, 90
Mensheviks, 49, 54, 66, 80, 95, 97
Mercader, Caridad, 152
Mercader, Jaime Ramon Hernandez del Rio, 152, 181
Mexican Communist Party, 146
Mexico/Mexicans, 9, 10, 15, 146-148, 151. Coyoacan, 9, 148. Mexico City, 9, 146, 181. Tampico, 146
Mikoyan, Anastas, 179
Military Revolutionary Committee, 85, 87, 95, 100, 117
Minsk, 43, 44
Molotov, Vyacheslav, 150, 165, 169, 175, 178
Mongols (Tatars), 18, 19, 20
Montgomery, Bernard, 160
More, Sir Thomas, 24
Mornard, Jacques, 15
Moscow, 19, 23, 55, 59, 60, 72, 91, 92, 97, 100, 108, 109, 111, 113, 114, 119, 127, 128, 134, 137, 144, 147, 152-154, 160, 162, 163, 166, 167, 170, 171, 177, 179, 181, 183
Murmansk, 109
MVD, 168, 170

Narodniks. See V Narod
Nasser, Gamal Abdel, 180
Nazis, 154, 155, 159, 171
Neiman River, 153
Netherlands, 160
Neva River, 88, 91
Nevsky Prospect, 94, 103
New Economic Policy, 117, 119
Nixon, Richard, 179, 180
NKVD, 144, 146
Normandy, 158
North Atlantic Treaty Organization (NATO), 177
Northern Society, 26

October Manifesto, 57, 58
Odessa, 46, 54
OGPU, 138, 139, 144
Oleg, 17
Order Number One, 76, 77, 81
Order of Lenin, 152, 166-168

Pacific, war in, 162
Paris Summit Conference, 180, 181
Pearl Harbor, 154
People's Republic (Korea), 165
People's Will, The, 35, 36
Pero (The Pen), 45, 46
Pestel, Paul, 26, 27
Peter and Paul Fortress, 93
Petrograd, 22, 75, 78, 81-85, 87, 88, 92-95, 97, 99, 100, 102, 103, 108, 129
Petrovna, Nina. See Khrushchev, Nina
Plekhanov, George, 36, 38, 40, 42-45, 47-49, 54, 66, 69, 77, 80, 100
Poets Club, 30
Poland, 23, 107, 149, 151, 153, 158, 164, 175, 176
Politburo (Political Bureau), 85, 135, 136, 138, 139, 143, 147, 150, 168
Poltava, 47
Potemkin, 54
Potsdam Conference, 161
Pravda, 68, 150
Presidium, 168, 170, 172, 177-179, 183, 184
private property, abolition of, 96, 97, 108, 115
Protopopov, Minister of the Interior, 71, 72
Provisional Committee, 74
Provisional Government, 76, 78-80, 82-87, 89, 91, 97, 114, 133
Pugachev, Emilian, 23
Pugachev's Uprising, 23
Pulkovo, 99
purge trials, 144-149, 174

Rahja, Eino, 89
Railroad Union, 55
Rasputin, Gregory, 63-65, 68-72
Red Army, 110, 112, 115, 146, 149, 151, 155, 160, 172, 176
Red Guards, 84, 86, 90, 92-94, 100, 101, 109

Red Square, 128, 167, 184
Red Terror, 110
Renaissance, 20, 24, 25
Revolutions. 1848, 27. 1905, 53-60. 1917, Communist, 23, 87-94, 149
Ribbentrop-Molotov Pact, 150
Rivera, Diego, 146
Robins, Harold, 12-14
Rodzianko, 73, 74
Romanovs, Alexander 1, 25-27. Alexander II, 33, 35, 36. Alexander III, 36, 39, 41. Alix (Alexandra Feodorovna), 41, 48, 51, 63-65, 68, 70-76, 111, 112. Catherine 1, 22. Catherine II (The Great), 22-25. Constantine, 27. Elizabeth, 27. Michael, 20. Michael, Grand Duke, 74. Nicholas I, 27, 28, 32, 33. Nicholas II, 41, 42, 48, 50-53, 56-58, 61-65, 68-76, 94, 100, 111, 112; children, 51, 63-65, 112. Nicholas, Grand Duke, 56, 57, 70, 71. Paul, 23, 25. Peter I (The Great), 20-23, 129, 155. Peter III, 22, 23
Rome/Romans, 24
Roosevelt, Franklin D., 156, 158, 159, 161
rota system, 18
Rumania, 54, 160, 164
Rurik, 17
Russian Orthodox Church/priests, 50, 100
Russian Social Democratic Labor Party, 43, 47, 58, 66, 67, 69, 100, 108

St. Petersburg, 22, 34, 39, 40, 43, 47, 48, 50, 52, 55, 58, 72-75, 129
satellite countries. See by individual names
Scandinavia, 17
schools, 116
serfs, 18, 21-23, 26, 33. emancipation of, 33
Sevastopol, 56
Siberia, 21, 26, 43-45, 47, 63, 67, 68, 77, 142, 147, 158, 178
Simbirsk, 39
Smolny Institute, 87-89, 91, 92, 94

socialism, 24. scientific, 32. utopian, 32

Social Revolutionaries, 47, 62, 80, 95, 97, 104, 105, 114

South Russia Workers Union, 46

Southern Society, 26

Soviets, Ekaterinburg, 112. Leningrad, 135, 143. Moscow, 59, 85, 100, 116, 121. Petrograd, 76, 77, 79-81, 84, 85, 87, 89-91, 95-97, 100. St. Petersburg, 55, 57, 58, 61, 74

Soviet Exhibition of Science and Technology, 179

Stalin, Ekaterina, 67

Stalin, Joseph, 9, 10, 15, 66-68, 77, 85, 88, 97, 110, 111, 120-138, 140, 141, 143, 145, 146, 148-153, 156, 158-162, 164-168, 170, 172, 174-176, 178

Stalingrad, 129, 156

State Council, 62, 72

Summit Conference. See Paris Summit Conference

Supreme Military Tribunal, 144-146

Supreme Soviet, 172, 178, 181, 184

Switzerland, 42-44, 69, 73. Geneva, 36, 38, 45, 49, 53, 54. Zurich, 77

Tatars. See Mongols

Teheran Conference, 156

Thirty-eighth parallel, 164

Tiflis, 67

Til (Lenin's chauffeur), 113

Timashuk, Dr. Lydia, 166, 168

Time of Troubles, 20

Tito, Marshall, 160

Treaties: Brest-Litovsk, 108, 151. with Germany, 149, 150, 152, 153. with Japan, 153, 158. test ban, 183

Trotsky, Leon, 9-16, 46-48, 53, 56-58, 61, 66, 68, 73, 77, 80-82, 84, 85, 87-92, 95, 97, 99, 101, 106, 110-112, 119, 122, 125-129, 131-139, 143, 145-149, 151, 152, 174, 181. children: Lyev, 139, 145, 147, 148. Nina, 147. Sergei, 139, 140, 145, 147. Zina, 147. grandson, Seva, 9, 14, 148

Trotsky, Natalia, 9-14, 139, 145-148, 181

Truman, Harry S., 161, 163

Tsars. See Romanovs

Tsaritsyn, 110, 129

Tsarskoye Selo, 75, 88, 100

Turkey, 23, 107

Ukraine, 107, 108, 115, 149-151, 153, 154, 158, 159

Ulyanov, Alexander (Sasha), 39, 40

Ulyanov, Madame, 39, 40

Ulyanov, Maria, 117-120, 122, 126

Ulyanov, Vladimir. See Lenin

Union of Salvation (Union of Welfare), 26

Union of Unions, 54

United Nations, 158, 159, 164, 165, 176

United States of America/Americans, 91, 108, 109, 115, 118, 147, 150, 152, 154, 159, 161, 163-166, 169, 172, 177, 179-183. New York 77

Ural Mountains, 155

Utopia, 25

U-2 incident, 180, 181

Vietnam, North, 182

Vishinsky, Andrei, 144, 147

Vladivostok, 109

V Narod (Narodniks), 34

Voroshilov, Klim, 134

Vyborg Manifesto, 65

Warsaw Pact, 177

Washington, D.C., 158

Wehrmacht, 153, 155

White Army/Guards, 100, 108-112, 114, 115

Winter Palace, 50-52, 62, 90-93

Women's Battalion, 91

Workers' University, 171

World War I, 69-74, 77-85, 96, 97, 107, 108, 114, 115, 171

World War II, 10, 153-160, 162, 171, 172

Yagoda, 146

Yalta, 158, 162

Yanovsky, 56

Yaroslav, 18, 19

Yeshov, 146, 148, 149

Yugoslavia, 160, 172, 177

zemstvos, 33, 54

Zinoviev, Gregory, 66, 68, 83, 85, 91, 124, 130-132, 134-138, 140, 143-146, 174

About the Author

KAYE MOULTON TEALL was born in Wichita, Kansas. She did her undergraduate work at the University of Wichita and at the University of Oklahoma, where she received her bachelor's degree and a Social Studies teaching certificate. She has done graduate work in Asian Studies at the East-West Center, on the campus of the University of Hawaii. Mrs. Teall began her professional career as a radio writer, doubling as an announcer on women's news and homemaking hints. She also has worked as a writer-producer for an advertising agency, and has done free-lance public relations. But the job she likes best is the one she is doing now: teaching history. She is currently employed as a television teacher for Channels 13 and 25, the educational stations in Oklahoma City, Oklahoma. Mrs. Teall writes both fiction and non-fiction and finds time for her writing during vacations.